Cinderella Square

A History of Portland Square

Bette Burke

Had I but plenty of money, money enough and to spare
The house for me, no doubt, were a house in the city square

Robert Browning

CONTENTS

Introduction

PORTLAND SQUARE, situated to the north of Broadmead, Bristol's main shopping area, is reputed to be the most complete of the city's eighteenth century squares. Despite this distinction many Bristolians remain unaware of its existence.

One reason for this is that the square enjoyed only a relatively short period as a fashionable place of residence before falling into decline. For more that a hundred years and especially after the Second World War, when it suffered extensive bomb damage, Portland Square became derelict and uninviting.

I first came into contact with the square in 1971 when my husband's wholesale business was relocated to No. 25. In 1986 we took up residence in the top floor flat and became the first people to live in the square for many years.

The deeds of the building made fascinating reading and I thought I might one day write its history. However, it was not until the restoration of No. 27 carried out so lovingly by June Burrough, that I decided to research the entire square.

The records disclosed the very chequered history of this Georgian masterpiece and within the last few years a move has been made to revitalise the square, adding to its already established commercial interests a new residential and cultural dimension.

Bette Burke, Bristol, September 2004.

CHAPTER ONE

Foundations

BRISTOL, AT THE END OF THE EIGHTEENTH CENTURY, was England's second city and an important seaport. Rich in trade its inhabitants had begun to demand an architecture which would reflect their wealth and position.

The Industrial Revolution was having a huge influence on the movement of agricultural workers, drawing them away from the land into the towns and cities and this inevitably led to an increase in urbanisation and a surge in building activity. Another consequence of this demographic movement was that churches were becoming unable to house their growing congregations.

Such was the case with the Church of St. James, which served the parishioners of St. James's Square and its surroundings. (St. James's Square was demolished in a bombing raid during World War II). An Indenture dated the 29th September 1787 stated that the Church of St. James was 'too inadequate to house the numerous inhabitants of that Parish and therefore an Act of Parliament was required for dividing that Parish and providing a separate Church, Cemetery and Parsonage house'.

The role of Parliament in the eighteenth century was far more parochial than is the case today. Several Acts were passed which dealt either directly or indirectly with the square but which today would come under the aegis of a central or local planning department.

There was some resistance to the proposal by a number of the church elders, but in the winter of 1787 the Corporation of Bristol approved the division of the Parish and the building of a new church and undertook to pay for the necessary Act of Parliament. The Act was passed in the same year and gave the Church Commissioners permission to buy land on which to build a church and parsonage. It also permitted them to sell any 'overplus ground'.

The Commissioners were faced with the task of finding a suitable site and a plot of land known as Barr's Leaze was investigated. This strip of land was an area of garden ground no more than 700 yards or so from St. James's Church, most of which belonged to the Dean and Chapter of Bristol. It measured six and three-quarter acres and was occupied by labourers who squatted the land and eked an existence from allotments and market gardening. Although it was so close to the existing church prospective residents were enthusiastic for a church of their own. A degree of snobbery was a major factor but also a new church would undoubtedly put up house prices.

Barr's Leaze seemed the obvious choice and the land and its occupants would have been cleared with little difficulty. The surplus land was sold as a speculative development and a grand square was envisaged to be named after the Duke of Portland, High Steward of Bristol at the time. Although the largest part of the land was the property of the Dean and Chapter of Bristol the ground on the west side was owned jointly by John Cave, an oil-colour merchant from Bristol and William Pritchard of Ross on Wye in Herefordshire. The names of these landholders were given to the side streets around the square. All traces of this area known as Barr's Leaze have disappeared save for Barrs Court. This is a walkway connecting Bond Street with the Horsefair.

The foundation stone of St Paul's Church was laid on April 23rd, 1789 and the church was consecrated in September 1794. One of the benefactors was a man named Thomas Dunckerley. He was a Freemason, as were many of those connected with this venture, and he donated a large sum towards the construction of the church.

Thomas Dunckerley was born in 1724 and in 1760 he discovered that he was the 'natural' son of King George II. It is possible that, the King having died in that year, Dunckerley's mother felt that it was time the facts were made known. Although the circumstances of this revelation were rather mysterious, the response to the information by King George III is well documented. He made a provision of £100 to Dunckerley, followed by a pension of £800 p.a. He was also given the use of rooms at Somerset House and later an apartment in Hampton Court Palace.

Among the many dignitaries at the ceremony in 1789 was the Mayor of Bristol, Levi Ames, whose gravestone can be seen in the graveyard behind the Unitarian Church in Brunswick Square.

As early as 1662 the classical square had become a fashionable and exclusive form of urban development. However, it was only London which had an upper class of sufficient size and wealth to sustain the building of residential squares. It was not until the beginning of the eighteenth century that the provinces were able to follow this trend and by 1750 Bristol could boast of five such squares, more than any other provincial town.

There was little aristocratic influence in Bristol architecture at this time as the city's upper class was almost totally composed of merchants. Consequently, building was conservative in design due to the dominance of local architects and masons who had little understanding of the new classical style which was sweeping London and Bath.

There appears to be some uncertainty as to which architect or architects were responsible for the design of both the church and the surrounding houses. Some favour William Paty who seems to be the only Bristol architect with Royal Academy training and who, together with his father Thomas and brother John, designed many of the city's elegant squares and terraces, including Berkeley Square and Charlotte Street.

The second name to emerge is that of Daniel Hague who appears to be most strongly linked to the square. A mason by trade he was also considered to be a proficient architect. A notice in the Bristol Journal of 1789 advertised the sale of building plots 'near the site of the new Church of St. Paul, plans of which with the elevations may be seen at Daniel Hague's, Architect and Builder in Wilder Street'. Unfortunately, the only architect's drawings to survive of the square are unsigned. Stylistic comparison with other work by Hague is difficult as no drawings which are definitely attributable to him are known to survive. He is said to have designed the Bristol Royal Infirmary with Paty but it is probable that the contract was solely for masonry work. The only other buildings in the city which are thought to be by Hague are Hope Chapel in Hope Chapel Hill, built in 1788, and Ashley Place, begun in 1790. However, this attribution is only based on stylistic comparison with Portland Square.

A third figure appears to complicate the matter still further. The rector of St. James's, the Rev. Joseph Atwell Small DD, was, like many vicars of the time, interested in designing his new church.

The City Council, however, who had put up £1,000 towards the building appointed a rival architect, James Allen, who had designed a church in the 'Grecian' style. After the submission of two separate tenders from builders, Allen's design was rejected on the grounds that it was too expensive and the commission was given to Hague. It was rumoured that some chicanery had taken place involving Dr. Small, whereby if Hague were willing to allow the Rector a hand in his design then his reward would be the design of Portland Square.

All this is pure conjecture and unless and until more evidence emerges to verify one or other position the mystery will remain. It is, however, interesting to compare the views of contemporary architects as to the true creator of this unique square.

Gordon Priest in *The Paty Family*, states that 'the metropolitan grandeur and distinct Adamesque flavour of Portland Square almost demands William Paty's involvement.....indeed Daniel Hague was a jobber and not capable of such sophistication unaided'.

Timothy Mowl in *To Build the Second City*, maintains that 'Daniel Hague's Portland Square marks an even more decisive move towards London fashions here at the north-east side of the city than William Paty's Park Street. What is, however, typically Bristolian, is that among the long horizontals of its houses, built to Hague's original modish designs stands the brilliant vertical of St. Paul's church, also by Hague'.

Somewhat earlier in 1952 Walter Ison in *The Georgian Buildings of Bristol*, equivocated by stating that 'Daniel Hague designed the church and square but that he may have been assisted by Paty and sons'.

One thing is certain, however, that the church, affectionately known as the 'Wedding Cake' church is one of Bristol's best loved landmarks.

The new fashions in architecture were embraced with great enthusiasm. Squares were frequently designed as the setting for a church or large house and uniformity came to be considered an essential element and was often used as a selling point. Although the open space in the centre of the square was at first surrounded by wooden posts to keep out carriages, it was quickly realised that a garden with shrubs and trees and perhaps a statue would be far more desirable and so it was with Portland Square.

Building in eighteenth century England was a speculative process, whereby the landholder or ground landlord leased a plot of land to a builder in return for a ground rent. The builder would build a house or houses or other premises and then lease them on. At the end of the term of the lease, the land with the buildings on it returned to the landholder. The landholder could never lose in this situation. He or she received ground rent during the term of the lease and the land which was eventually returned was, of course, greatly increased in value. In Bristol land was commonly leased in perpetuity, but if the annual ground rent was not paid the land and buildings reverted to the landholder. The building lease was to ensure that the building was completed within a fixed period, usually not longer than three years. This was to prevent the builder mortgaging his interest in the land and using the money gained for other purposes. In small schemes the landholder employed an architect or surveyor to draw up plans and elevations and lay down specifications as to dimensions, materials and standards of construction.

In the case of larger building schemes such as Portland Square and its side streets the landholder would lease to a building undertaker or middleman. Because of the greater expense of such schemes and the higher financial risks involved these were generally partnerships of a wealthy tradesman who would provide the finance together with one or more building craftsmen. Towards the end of the eighteenth century these partnerships would often include an attorney.

The Commissioners of St. Paul's first advertised the square for sale in June 1789 as building plots 'subject to yearly Fee Farm Rents and Covenants for building'. The ground had been staked out for building early in the previous year. The plots were originally to be auctioned in July 1789 but the auction was postponed and the development was not finally sold until April 1790. Most of the building plots were bought by a building and timber merchant named James Lockier, who was one of the largest building speculators in Bristol at that time. In partnership with him were Henry Cooke, sail maker, who was also his son-in-law, Thomas Pope, builder and John Cornish, City Gentleman. The Church Commissioners leased thirty building plots to James Lockier and his partners at a total yearly rent of £105. Building covenants were set up to ensure that Hague's designs would be adhered to, thus guaranteeing a fine setting for their church and maintaining the consistency of the square so important both for the image and the value of their investment.

Lockier and his partners bought the whole of the north, south and southwest sides of the square, the northwest side except for plot 34 which was probably developed by a member of the Cave family and five plots on the east side. They then sub-leased these plots to smaller builders: Thomas Pope, who contracted to build at least Nos. 27 and 28; the building partnership of Thomas Davies and John Husband who probably undertook to build six houses including Nos. 23 and 24; Thomas Blake who began Nos. 29 and 31 and may perhaps have built all of the northwest side, apart from 34; and the partnership of Thomas Lewis and Thomas Mitchell who started 5 Portland Square. The men were all local craftsmen. Each builder was to be responsible for paving and maintaining the footpath and for making a roadway in front of the plots they had leased. They also had to pay towards laying the common sewer and railing in and laying out the central garden.

The houses, although their interiors were not identical, were to be lavishly appointed and were to cost no less that £1000 to build, a huge amount at the time. They were to be of stone or brick and ornamentally fronted with freestone. Roofs were to be covered in Cornish slates or in lead. Slate was expensive but would have been chosen for its durability and resistance to water as well as its appearance. The rooms were to be large and there would, of course, be servants' quarters as well as coach houses. No. 28 was advertised in August 1793 as having a complete range of servants' offices, a coach house capable of holding two carriages and stables for six horses. Entry into the coach house was by means of a service arch or bridge. No. 27 is the only house in the square which still retains these original outbuildings.

The high hopes for the enterprise were thwarted by the outbreak of the Napoleonic Wars. These upheavals precipitated a crisis of confidence in investment in the building industry and in May 1793 Lockier was declared bankrupt. It seems that he had overreached himself earlier in other speculative ventures and he and his backers were fighting to keep their projects afloat. Unfortunately, their failure to do this brought down virtually all of the smaller tradesmen associated with him, including Pope and Davies and Husband.

Although building was well underway by then, the plots in the square with their unfinished houses reverted to Lockier and between August 1793 and April 1794 they were sold off to pay his creditors. Despite the financial crisis there seem to have been no lack of buyers, two of whom, William Sheppard and James Chapman, bought a substantial amount of property in the area.

Partly because of the disruption caused by the French Wars and partly because it was in any case fairly usual for large and expensive speculative building projects to take some time to complete, the square was not finally finished until about 1823 and not fully inhabited until 1825. Three sides of the square though, the north, west and east seem from ratebook evidence to have been substantially completed by 1811.

Without access to the deeds of a property it is virtually impossible to ascertain whether the owner lived in the house or had acquired it as an investment. In the case of No. 25 the deeds show that this particular property as well as others in the square was bought by Samuel Henderson, a wealthy sugar merchant. After his death in 1815 his property was shared between his two granddaughters, Mary Ann Henderson and Mary Ludlow Henderson. The husband of Mary Ann Henderson, Sir Frederick Fowke of Scraptoft in Leicestershire is listed in the ratebooks as the owner of No. 28. There is no evidence in the Directories of the period that this family ever resided in the square.

Many houses in the square appear to have been rented to one or more occupants, a few having as many as three families sharing a property. The Directories supply the name, address and occasionally the occupation of the entrants. However, it is only where the title 'proprietor' appears in the entry that one can be sure of the ownership.

Bristol had no piped water supply until 1846 so the residents of Portland Square would have obtained their water supplies from both ground and rain water. There would have been pumps in the yard at the rear of the basement floor and in fact No. 27 has a well in the basement. The risk of contamination from the proximity of the drains would have been fairly high. There would also have been lead rain-water cisterns.

There were 'water closets' in the better type of Georgian house and these would certainly have been installed in all of the properties in Portland Square, although their lack of ventilation and uncertain operation made it advisable to separate them from the house if possible. When giving advice to architects, Isaac Ware wrote '.... a water closet, far removed and connected by a passage is a good thing'. Toilets would have had a cistern valve to keep a constant level of water in the pan and flushed from a cistern set into the wall behind. The water would have been supplied either from a rainwater tank on the roof or pumped from below, draining through the back of the house into a brick drain. The main drain, with cesspits set along it and running under the middle of the building would have joined the common sewer in the square. Bristol's sewage at the time ran directly into the River Avon.

Advertisements are an extremely rich source of information regarding the dimensions of living rooms and the layout of both these room and the service quarters. One such advertisement for No. 22 in 1814 lists two large arched cellars, a servants hall, a large coal cellar and other offices on the area floor or basement. The 1816 advertisement adds a wine cellar. Coal was often stored in vaults built under the streets at the front of the building and conveniently filled through a hole in the pavement, covered with a block of stone or iron. A number of these can still be seen around the square.

On the ground floor, No. 22 is advertised as having an entrance hall, a front parlour 21 ft. by 25 ft., a back parlour and a china pantry, a cook's kitchen and brewhouse with an upper floor and a garden. However, the garden would not have been a leisure area but would probably have housed a pump for groundwater.

No. 28 has an entrance hall and the ground floor room at the front of the building has the same dimensions as the front parlour in No. 22. This room may have been used as a dining room as it was close to the service stairs and kitchens. The drawing room above was used as a receiving room as it was the custom to entertain visitors on the first floor, possibly away from the noise and smell from the street below. On the second floor of No. 22 there were four bedrooms and a water closet and the third floor also had four bedrooms. Some of the bedrooms on this floor may have been set aside as servants quarters.

One of the few houses in the square which still boasts most of the original internal features is No. 27, including marble fireplaces with fluted friezes and panels and inlays of various colours and beautiful decorated ceiling cornices. However, the most spectacular feature is the staircase with its mahogany handrail and curved newel post, sweeping vertically through the entire structure and above which is a conical lantern decorated with plaster baskets of fruit. The house was built for the attorney, William Daniel, and contrary to the fashionable custom of the time he decided to receive his guests in the ground floor front parlour and dine them in the room behind.

There is no evidence available to show how the roofs of the Portland Square houses might have been arranged. However, an aerial photograph taken in 1921 shows the plan of the roof of No. 28 to be much as it is today. The roof is hipped with a north/south ridge covering the front rooms of the house and the hallway, except for the stair well, and a flat roof at the rear. A chimney stack rises through the party wall with No. 27. The photograph shows a hexagonal structure on the flat roof which appears to be attached to the central section of the pitched roof over the hallway. This seems to suggest that the house may originally have had a roof garden or conservatory. Roof gardens were quite common in Georgian town houses and the conservatories would be filled with pot plants and ornamented with architectural features. The roofs in Portland Square would have commanded fine views over the city and the surrounding countryside.

These conservatories would have provided a splendid amenity for star gazing, which was a popular pastime in the nineteenth century. Unfortunately, Bristol at that time was suffering from the effects of its increasing industry and manufacture. Plentiful supplies of coal from mines in the Forest of Dean and elsewhere in the region were a stimulus to a number of local industries.

One of the main industries was the manufacture of glass. There were twelve glass houses in the city and their production was higher than anywhere else in the country. They produced glass bottles for Hotwell's Water, Cider, Perry and Wine, as well as window glass. Other industries included the production of lead shot, brass manufacture and porcelain.

So much industry did have its drawbacks in that it polluted the atmosphere and, in some cases, poisoned the soil. On calm days the air in the Avon valley could be stifling and acrid and smoke from the factory chimneys could keep the city in almost impenetrable obscurity. Star gazers would have had to wait for a strong westerly wind to clear the air.

This description of Bristol was possibly a little misleading as there were many unpolluted areas in the city, Queen's Square, the Avon Gorge and, of course, Portland Square.

The aspirations of all those concerned in this venture, the landholders, architects, builders and residents were for a setting comparable with those in London and Bath. The dignified elegance of the square with its classical features and imposing Gothic church ensured that, albeit for a short time, an address in the Square was the very height of fashion.

CHAPTER TWO

A Leisurely Life Style

ADAPTATIONS ON TELEVISION AND FILM OF THE NOVELS OF JANE Austen and other eighteenth century writers have tended to portray Georgian England as a rural idyll, a country whose inhabitants were undisturbed either by revolution or by the noise of traffic or industry.

Historical evidence, however, provides us with a very different view of society and Bristol bore its share of unrest. Quite apart from the riots in 1831 and the sacking of Queen's Square, an incident occurred in Portland Square which, although not so momentous an event, was considered sufficiently newsworthy to be reported in *Felix Farley's Bristol Journal.*

The residents of the square had decided to order a statue of King George III to commemorate his 50th Jubilee in 1809. Unfortunately, the statue was not ready in time and an obelisk was put up temporarily in the garden on 28th October, 1809.

An advertisement was placed in *Felix Farley's Bristol Journal* on 14th October, 1809:

> ***TO ALL MASONS***
>
> *The Plan of an OBELISK to be erected by SUBSCRIPTION, in PORTLAND SQUARE, in honour of His MAJESTY, who enters in the 50th Year of his Reign on the 25th of the present Month, will be laid in the Vestry Room, St.Paul's, on MONDAY next, for the Inspection of those Masons, who are willing to give an estimate for Building the same.*
>
> *JOHN USHER, Clerk of the Vestry.*
> *P.S. Subscriptions may be sent to any Gentleman of the Vestry.*

The statue itself was to be made of Coade stone and the sculpture has been attributed to Joseph Panzetta. It was probably just over life-size and was finally erected in the centre of the garden in April 1810 and inscribed with the words:

> 'George The Third, the Father of his People, having on 25th October, 1809, through the Favour of Divine Providence, attained the 50th Year of his Reign – to commemorate that happy event, and in testimony of their Gratitude for the Blessings enjoyed under the mild Government of the best of Kings, the loyal inhabitants of St. Paul's Parish erected this Statue'
>
> A.D. 1810

Unfortunately, these sentiments were not shared by all the King's subjects. In March 1813 the Journal stated that a radical agitator, by the name of Henry 'Orator' Hunt, made an inflammatory speech outside the Exchange in Corn Street in favour of the Princess of Wales, (Princess Caroline) and against the Prince of Wales. That same evening a group of eight or nine men entered Portland Square and, by means of a rope, toppled the statue. It fell with a tremendous crash, alarming the inhabitants and broke in many pieces. It has never been replaced. One of the men arrested, John Harris, was sentenced to a year's imprisonment in Newgate and fined forty shillings.

Although the Parish of St. Paul's was a 'leafy suburb' far from the noise and smells of the city, there would have been little peace or tranquillity for the residents.

Nearly all the households in the square kept a carriage and horses, and as we have seen No. 28 had the capacity for two carriages. Rubber tyres were not introduced until late in the nineteenth century so that the iron wheels and horses hooves striking against the cobbled streets would have created an unimaginable cacophony. Add to this the noise of the carts delivering coal and provisions, as well as street vendors selling their produce, then perhaps a true picture of the square in all

To be sold by Auction

BY Mr Stephens,

At No 1 PORTLAND SQUARE

On MONDAY the 9th July, and following days,

The Elegant and HIghly FASHIONABLE BED-ROOM, DRAWING ROOM, EATING-ROOM, PARLOUR nand other FURNITURE, Large Collection of Tab;e and Tea CHINA, Cut and Plain GLASS, Library of BOOKS in the richest bindings, the whole the property of the Gentleman deceased.

The bedrooms comprise mahogany four-post bedsteads, with superfine chintz cotton furniture lined with calico, and window curtains to correspond, bordered paleas; mattresses, prime seasoned goose feather beds; large blankets and counterpanes; mahogany commode chests of drawers; dressing and night tables.

The Drawing-room - superb sofa, and elbow mahogany chairs in red morocco and brass-nailed, with fine medallion cases, card, Pembroke and pier tables; large pier glasses in burnished frames; capital double-branch cut lustres; superfine chintz cotton French window curtains; Brussels carpet, fitted; fine mirror.

In the Eating-room - highly polished mahogany sideboard with brass rail; set of dining-tables; 30 inch mirror in gold frame; mahogany chairs in purple morocco brass-nailed,; card tables, sopha with cotton case; French window curtains; Brussels carpet,etc

The Parlour - large mahogany library range, fitted in the most complete manner; lambour writing table; large pier glasses; mahogany chair in purple morocco, brass nailed; card tables; chintz cotton French window curtains; Brussels carpet fitted; an exceeding fine bracket clock, on mahogany pedestal.

The kitchens and offices are replete with useful furniture.

Catalogues may be had after 2nd July by applying t the auctioneer at 16 Cumberland Street.

To be viewed the Thursday and Friday preceding the days of sale from Ten in the morning till Four in the afternoon.

The sale to commence each morning at TEN.

Felix Farley's Bristol Journal, Saturday June 16 1804

its vibrancy may begin to emerge.

In 1851 there were thirty children under the age of fifteen living in Portland Square. By 1861, perhaps as a result of Queen Victoria's burgeoning family, the number had increased to fifty eight. This would have called for a formidable army of nursemaids to manage these large families. Each day the girls, often very young and always impeccably dressed in starched uniforms, would parade their perambulators through the garden, no doubt passing on the gossip picked up 'below stairs'.

The garden would probably have looked much as it does today, although the trees would have been newly planted. This would have given a clear view across the square of the church and houses, which was presumably what the architect intended.

Before the introduction of gas lighting, streets were dark and dangerous places at night. By 1818 the gas lamp had been perfected and demand was such that it was considered imperative to install the gas network as soon as possible. However, a conflict arose between the companies laying the mains and erecting the lamp-standards and the interests of the Paving Commissioners. A further Act of Parliament was necessary and this was passed in March 1819 which resolved the situation. Gas lighting for both public and private use was introduced to the city of Bristol including the Parish of St. Paul's.

The first residents of the square consisted mainly of professional men and their families, an assortment of attorneys, surgeons, physicians, clergymen and bankers. Several residents described themselves as gentlemen, presumably living off investments and annuities. There were also a number of merchants.

William Wilberforce's anti-slavery bill of 1792 had seen the end of that trade in Bristol by the turn of the century but the main products of the plantations, tobacco and sugar, helped to provide the basis of the city's overseas trade. They also reflected the merchandise of several of those merchants living in Portland Square.

Perhaps the most illustrious resident of the square was Henry Overton Wills, the founder of the tobacco firm W.D. & H.O Wills. In 1815 he moved from his house on Redcliffe Hill to No. 2 Portland Square. The house had twelve rooms and the price paid was £1475.00 with additional furniture costing a further £128.00. However one of his grandsons, H.O. Wills III remarked that when his grandfather bought the house only one man in the square besides himself did not drive a coach and pair, H.O. Wills I having but one horse.

The Wills family were associated with the square for many years. Records show that in 1841, William D. Wills, aged 43 lived at No. 2 with his London born wife, Mary, aged 54 and ten year old son Frederick. By 1871, W.D. Wills had died, Frederick had moved on but Mary, now aged eighty-four, was still in residence. Living on independent means with three servants and a footman, the one horse had, by necessity, been upgraded to a coach and pair.

Another member of the Wills family lived in the square for a short while. In 1855, W.H. Wills aged 30, lived at No. 6 but by 1857 he had moved to No. 9. Unfortunately he had left the square before the next census in 1861 so it is not possible to give details of his family. H.O.Wills II had twenty children by his two wives, so it is reasonable to suggest that W.H. Wills was one of them.

Two sugar merchants lived in the square, both having taken up residence in 1815. The families lived next door to each other, William Harwood at No. 16 dealt in raw sugar and Thomas Beddoe at No. 17 was a sugar refiner. Perhaps their mutual interests had led to friendship.

William Harwood lived at No. 16 from 1815 until his possible death in 1840 when the house passed to a surgeon, Henry Cuznor. He lived there for nine years and in 1850 Thomas Hawkins, also a surgeon, took up residence with his wife Jane. Thomas was forty-two years of age at the time and his wife was eleven years his junior. His father,

Thomas Hawkins senior, was a druggist and lived at No. 6 Newfoundland Street. With his son moving into Portland Square, we can see this as an example of upward mobility, living in the square in 1850 was a definite statement of success.

By 1861 Thomas and Jane had four children between the ages of eight and four. Ten years later Thomas Hawkins was a widower with five children between nine and eighteen years, employing one domestic servant. It is possible that his wife had died in childbirth, a major cause of death in Victorian England. The children are all listed as scholars and, in fact, two of the sons became surgeons. The last entry for this family is in 1881, which records William Hawkins, surgeon, attended by a domestic servant and a page aged sixteen years.

There are several houses in the square which remained family homes for a number of generations. Nos. 2 and 16 must certainly have been happy places to live and No. 17 seems even more so. The Beddoe family occupied this house from 1815 until 1885.

Thomas Beddoe had three children. The eldest was a daughter, Ann, then came two sons, twins, born two years later, neither of whom carried on their father's trade. Henry Beddoe was an attorney and Thomas A. Beddoe became an iron founder. In 1832 the house was listed under the name of Henry with the father as retired. By 1851 just Thomas and his sister were listed, with two domestic servants. The brother and sister remained together until in 1881 they took in a lodger. By then they were eighty-six and eighty-eight years of age.

Thomas A. Beddoe's trade as an iron founder reflects one of the local industries at than time. As we have seen there were iron and lead as well as glass factories in and around Bristol and money was to be made by enterprising manufacturers and merchants.

There seems to have been only one resident dealing in china and glass in the square. William Payne lived at No. 6 with his wife, Jane and their six children from 1851 until 1855. There were two sons aged eighteen and sixteen years and four daughters aged fifteen, nine, seven and five years. They employed one cook and one domestic.

There were, however, three dealers in metals; Thomas Hooper Riddle, together with his son, Herbert, were lead merchants and lived at No. 14 from 1825 until 1845, Jasper Westcott, brass founder and copper-smith lived at No. 20 from 1835 until 1851 and Francis A. Barnett, who made wrought iron and brass bedsteads. He lived at No. 5 from 1850 until 1856 with his wife, Mary and their two sons. They employed two domestic servants. This is possibly not an accurate account of the tradespeople living in the square as a number of the residents are listed simply as merchants.

The square was obviously a successful place for doctors and surgeons. At No. 29 Dr. William Ogilvie Porter, physician, remained happily ensconced for thirty-five years, from 1815 until 1850 when he was seventy-four years old.

William had been a naval surgeon before coming to the square and he was a member of a most talented family. His sister Jane, who also lived at No. 29, was a gifted authoress. She wrote many books, among which were *The Scottish Chiefs* and *Thaddeus of Warsaw*. Walter Scott admitted that her work was the inspiration of the *Waverley* novels. Another sister, Anna Maria, who lived in Montpelier, also wrote romantic fiction. Her novel *The Hungarian Brothers* written in 1807, was a popular success.

Their brother, Sir Robert Ker Porter, was an artist and in 1804 he secured the appointment of historical painter to the Czar of Russia. He fell in love with a Russian princess but was forced to leave Russia because of this involvement. He decided to cover the Peninsular War in Spain and became one of the first war painters. In 1811 he revisited Russia and married his princess.

In 1855 a surgeon named William Ormerod moved into No. 19. He was fifty-eight years of age and his family included his wife, Harriet, who was ten years younger and their three children, a son and two daughters. The records show that in 1861 the family were still there. The son, William George, was then thirty years old and he too had become a surgeon. The two daughters were aged twenty and eighteen years. The family employed one domestic servant and a page. In 1871, the house was listed under the name of William George who shared the house with his eldest sister, both of whom were unmarried.

Five years later No. 19 was occupied by yet another surgeon, Charles Newman MRCS, LRCP. In 1881 the census shows that, at the age of thirty one, he had married Harriet who was twenty three years old. Also living with them were Charles' father, Joseph aged seventy five years and his sister, Charlotte aged thirty years and unmarried. They employed two domestic servants. In 1891 the family was still there, with the addition of two children. They now employed a cook, a housemaid and a nurse.

In 1901 a medical surgeon from Dublin, named Philip McCrea aged thirty-five came to live in the house and he worked from home. He seemed to have had no family but employed two domestic servants. He remained there until 1910. Six years later No. 19 became the home of the Bristol Municipal Tuberculosis Dispensary.

There were a number of boarding schools situated in the square. The houses were large and could therefore accommodate a reasonable number of students. This type of establishment, especially for young girls, was extremely popular in the nineteenth century. The subjects on offer were designed to produce a woman of elegance and practical ability. Deportment was high on the agenda, together with musical instruction, perhaps a foreign language, needlework and a little cookery. Sadly, not all schools attained these high standards and many were there merely to relieve their overburdened parents, as, of course, there was no state schooling at that time.

One of the most successful schools in the square was that run by the

Misses Thomas. In 1825, Sarah and Emily Thomas, who were then just twenty three and twenty two years old respectively, established a Ladies Boarding School at No. 7. Just why these two young women should decide, at such an early age, to become governesses and devote themselves to teaching will never be revealed. The intimate details of the daily lives of the residents of Portland Square are, unfortunately, not recorded in any census and no letters or diaries appear to have survived. Suffice to say, that the two women decided that a Ladies School would enable them to enjoy a home and a means of livelihood under one roof in one of the most fashionable areas of Bristol.

This school was the largest in the square. In 1841 there were fourteen boarders aged between ten and fifteen years and in 1851, twelve students were recorded. To look after this household, there was just one cook and one domestic servant. The school continued until 1860, when the Misses Thomas retired and left the square.

There were other perhaps less successful boarding schools for young ladies in the square. At No. 25 Miss Rees ran a school from 1835 to 1841 and at No. 22 Marcia Phillippart opened a ladies school in 1850. Although her husband was a Professor of Languages, this school survived for only one year. Mrs. Sophia Parish ran a Ladies Boarding School at No. 15 between 1825 and 1832.

In 1851 Bertram Mack, the German Director of the Bristol Conservatoire of Music, came to live at No. 22 with his wife Eliza and their daughter. Also living at the house was another German musician, John Geramhausen, with his wife and son. It is not known whether No. 22 had actually become the Bristol Conservatoire or merely housed the staff. They remained there until 1861.

Another girls' boarding school at No. 15 was run by the Misses Holmes. Their mother, Harriet a widow, was head of the household in 1871 and was an annuitant. Her daughters, aged forty-four and forty-one years of age were both unmarried. They were schoolmistresses and had established a boarding school at the house. After their mother's death in 1874 the school continued but it was to last only a further two years.

No. 28 housed the Norman School. Robert Saunders was the Principal and in 1850 there were nine students recorded. Robert and his wife Anne employed a cook and a domestic servant. Also living in the house was their niece, aged seventeen years. It is not clear what her situation was, whether she helped teach or whether she was one of the students. The school was located in the square for only five years.

Portland Square was a magnet for the clergy. No. 18, which is situated on the northern side of the church, housed the vicars of St. Paul's, although the church hall lies behind No. 17 on the southern side. Rev. Small was the first incumbent and the church was served by twelve vicars until it finally closed in 1988.

Rev. Small finally retired in 1815, having served the church since its consecration in 1794. Rev. John Bull then became vicar and he remained there until 1822 when the post was taken up by Rev. James Olive. Three years later Rev. C.P. Bullock was installed as rector of St. Paul's until, in 1841 at the age of sixty-five, he retired and passed on his duties to Rev. Aaron Rogers who was forty-seven years of age. His wife, Ann, was two years younger and they had a daughter aged ten years and a son aged seven years. They employed a governess and two domestic servants. Rev. Rogers also remained at No. 18 until his retirement in 1868.

The sixth vicar of St. Paul's Church was Rev. C.S. Fripp. He was forty-five years of age when he took up his post, his wife being the same age. They had three children aged between one and thirteen years. Also living with them were three unmarried nieces, aged between fourteen and twenty-one years and three domestic servants. It is not clear why Rev. Fripp left No. 18 in 1876 as he was not of retirement age, but his place was taken by Rev. George Alford. He was fifty-two years of age at the time and his wife was four years his junior. They had four children between nine and seventeen years. They employed a parlourmaid, a cook and a housemaid.

In 1885 Rev. James Davidson B.A. became vicar. He was a widower and lived with his son who was a student of theology. The last four vicars recorded were Rev. F.G. Walmsley, 1915-1923, Rev. William Ward, 1923-1956, Rev. W.W. Orpwood, and lastly Rev. J.E. Viner, 1962.

There were, however, a large number of clergymen living in the square at various times who served other denominations in the city.

Rev. James Hollins was a minister of the Episcopalian Church and he lived at No. 4 from 1856 to 1876. He was married and had six children. The house continued to be a home for the clergy and in 1876 Rev. John Wadsworth took up residence. He remained there until 1891, when George Laws, a clerk in holy orders from London, moved in. He was married with two daughters aged four years and ten months. The family stayed until 1901.

Perhaps the most notable minister in the square was Rev. Samuel Emery Day, M.A., who lived at No. 32 with his wife and two children from 1841 until 1855. He then moved to No. 3 and lived there until his death in 1864.

Rev. Day was an Episcopalian and was the vicar of Ss. Philip and Jacob (known as Pip and Jay). He was the curate of that church between 1821 and 1832, acting for his father, Rev. William Day. At his father's death he became vicar and was the last minister to be appointed to the church by the Mayor and corporation.

The church commemorated both the father and son by a monument in the nave. A stained glass window was installed to the memory of Rev. S.E. Day and his portrait was hung in the vestry. Such was the respect felt by the city and corporation for Rev. Day that he was three times elected as chaplain to the Mayor.

His father, William, was also highly regarded and his funeral was attended, not only by nearly all the clergy of the established church, but also by many dissenting ministers resident in Bristol and its neighbourhood. As chaplain of Bristol gaol for twenty six years, he attended some of the city's most notorious criminals to the scaffold.

The residents of Portland Square found themselves the unwitting recipients of some notoriety when, on 4th June 1849, an exhumation took place in the churchyard of St.Paul's. The corpses of the wife and two children of a Kingsdown builder, T.W. Hill, were removed from their graves. Forensic tests proved that they had been poisoned with arsenic the previous autumn. Mr. Hill was set to receive £3000.00 from an insurance policy on his wife's life. Realising that his guilt would be discovered the builder took his own life by a dose of prussic acid, thus depriving the hangman and the citizens of Bristol of a public execution.

The railways featured fairly extensively in the square, either by direct employment or by pensions from shares. In 1871, Mr. Robert Nott moved into No. 29. He was a railway cashier from Taunton. His wife, Emma, was forty-three years old, seven years younger than her husband. Their son, William aged sixteen years, was a railway clerk and lived at home, together with his five brothers and sisters, aged between fourteen and eight years. They employed a governess and one domestic servant and there was also a lodger.

In 1881, the census shows that the family was still there. Robert had become a railway accountant and William, now aged twenty-six years, unmarried and living at home, was a city clerk. Two of their daughters, aged twenty-two and twenty-one years, also unmarried and living at home, were teachers and another son aged twenty was an assistant teacher. Robert and Emma had had another child, a daughter, who was seven years of age. A nephew had come to live with the family. He was also called Robert, and was an ironmonger's assistant. They kept one servant.

In 1832, William Hassell and family resided at No. 31, but by 1841 they had moved to No. 10. Both William and his youngest son, James, were leather factors. However, an older son, John, had a job as Landing Waiter at the Customs House. This must have been quite a prestigious post as his two sisters, Charlotte and Eliza, aged forty-three and thirty-eight years respectively in 1851, were financially independent through railway shares.

In 1861, No. 31 once more became the home of a railway employee, Henry Dykes, aged fifty-five years, who was a Superintendent of the Bristol Exeter Railway. He and his wife, Jane, had four daughters aged twenty-five, nineteen, eighteen and six years and two sons aged twenty-three and seventeen years. They kept one domestic servant, presumably the daughters helped with the chores. The elder son was an accountant and the younger, a clerk.

In 1871, the census shows that the family were still together, none of the children having married. In 1876, Jane was widowed and living on interest, probably of railway shares. By 1881, at the age of seventy-two she was sharing the house with three of her daughters. They continued to live there until 1885.

Bristol was the centre of a large agricultural area and this was reflected in the number of corn and flour merchants living in the square. William Baker lived at No. 27 from 1850 until 1856. He was a corn factor, maltster and hop merchant and in 1851 he and his wife had five sons, aged sixteen, twelve, eleven ten and eight years and two daughters, aged four and two years. William's mother-in-law, Mary Thomas, then aged eighty years, also lived with them, together with three domestic servants.

William Baker was in partnership with a Mr. Edwards and the firm of Baker & Edwards evidently flourished. In 1832 William was living at No. 12 Dean Street, St. Paul's with one business address, his 'counting house', in Stratton Street. By 1841 the partners had a second premises in Wilder Street. In 1850 their office was registered at No. 11 Welsh Back, which seems to have coincided with the move to Portland Square.

A flour factor named George Whitford, lived at No. 6 with his wife and an unmarried niece from 1861 until 1868. However, it was not until 1901 that a flour merchant once again took up residence in the house. Alfred Dennis lived at No. 6 with his wife, one daughter and two sons. In 1905 he decided to work from home as the Victoria Flour Company, which continued trading until 1958.

Corn and provision merchant, Francis Adams, lived at No. 9 with his wife and brother between 1850 and 1856. In 1861 a corn merchant named Henry Humphries lived at No. 34 with his wife and two daughters, aged twenty-three and twenty-five years together with a boarder aged sixteen years. He was possibly an apprentice. The family kept a cook and a housemaid.

A further example of upward mobility was flour salesman, William Kearsey, who moved from Wilson Street to No. 13 in 1868. He took with him his wife, six children, aged between seven and eighteen years and one domestic servant. The children were all listed as scholars. In 1885 there were four unmarried children, three daughters and a son still living in the house. One daughter was a governess and the son, aged twenty-seven, was an undergraduate. There were no servants so presumably the two daughters, listed as having no occupation, helped with the housework.

No. 14 was the home of William Greenslade, who was a corn and seed merchant. He lived there from 1845 until 1861 with his wife and three children. They also had a lodger and three domestic servants.

In 1841 a corn merchant by the name of John Shoard moved into No. 15. He was a partner in the company, Proctor and Shoard, who styled themselves as corn and flour millers. He remained at No. 15 for ten years. In 1856 William Balsdon, a seed, corn and hop factor took up residence but stayed for only four years.

One of the more amusing facts to come to light regarding the early residents of the square, was a family by the name of Stiff. They lived at No.19 between 1835 and 1855. Thomas Stiff, the head of the household, was a starch manufacturer.

There seems to be an intriguing situation at No. 21. In 1851 Mrs. H. Bailey, a widow aged sixty-nine years, is recorded as housekeeper. Living with her was a daughter, Mary, and her husband William Drake, who was a journeyman tailor. They had a daughter of nine months. Also living in the house was an unmarried daughter named Caroline. She was two years older than her sister and was a cloth cap maker. Records show that she had a son of six years whose name is recorded as Frederick Bailey. Unlike many unmarried women with children in Victorian England, she had not been forced to leave home but remained within her family circle.

A Professor in Botany named Samuel Rootsey moved into No. 25 in 1841 with his wife Eliza. There are no children recorded and there seems to be some confusion as to whether Samuel was still alive in 1851. It is not clear whether Eliza was wife or widow. However in that year the house was opened to lodgers. Two families took up residence, possibly those of father and son.

Henry Wheeler King, aged sixty-one years, was a solicitor and Henry Husband King, aged thirty-five years was a bookseller. There was also a male student, the wife of a timber merchant and the wife of a commercial traveller in ironmongery. Eliza kept two domestic servants and ran the lodging house at least until 1861 and possibly for a further ten years.

One resident with a highly colourful background was John Hamilton Clement. He was a metallingant (a term which has disappeared from common usage) and was the Superintendent of the Panther Lead Works. Born in Quebec, he travelled through Mexico and Merionethshire in Wales and finally came to live at No. 33 Portland Square. He had married a woman from Hammersmith in London, but there is no record as to where they met nor where they married. However, two of their daughters were born in Mexico and one in Wales. They had one domestic servant and one cook, both of whom were brought from Merionethshire. They arrived in the square in 1850 when John was forty-four years of age and his wife four years younger.

The Clements had left the square by 1855 and in 1861 Mr. Henry Guy, from Cornwall, moved into the house. He was also the manager of a lead smelting works but it is not possible to ascertain whether it was the same firm as that managed by John Clement. He and his wife, Ellen, had four children aged between ten and five years. Also living with them was Ellen's father, who was a retired master builder. They employed two domestic servants. Ten years later, the family were still there, the four children all living at home.

Portland Square was home to a number of close family households. Apart from the two Wills families mentioned earlier, brothers and fathers and sons seemed to enjoy the ambience of the square. Three attorneys all named Daniel lived in the square in the first quarter of the century; William, the original occupant of No. 27; Edward, who moved into No. 11 in 1815 and John, registered at No. 31. In 1825 Edward and John were both living at No. 11. They were presumably brothers but the records give no clue as to whether there was a relationship with the older William.

A family of hat manufacturers, named Dando, also occupied two houses in the square. In 1841 Joseph Dando, aged sixty years, lived at No. 26. His son, Charles, aged twenty-five years was at No. 13. Ten years later, on the death of his father, Charles moved into No. 26. At the age of thirty-six, no longer registered as a hatter but as a fund holder, Charles and his wife were living in grand style with a parlour maid, cook and domestic servant. They had two children, a son aged eight years and a daughter, a year younger. In 1861 Charles junior was studying to be an artist and the daughter had independent means. They still kept two domestic servants.

Two families named Bushell also lived two doors apart. In 1817, William Bushell moved into No. 9. He was an oil merchant and aged forty-six years. Little is known about his family but in the 1841 census he was still in the same house together with his son, Samuel aged thirty years. Also in this census, a merchant named William D. Bushell is recorded as living at No. 11. He was also thirty years old, but it is not clear whether he is a twin of Samuel or even related. The similarity of name does seem to be more than a coincidence.

We can see that, among the large families living in the square, many of the children remained unmarried. Perhaps there was little opportunity for them to meet suitable partners as travel to other towns must have been severely restricted. Men required substantial incomes before they could entertain marriage and the burden of so many children which would inevitably follow.

For a single woman, whose parents were still alive, the possibility of moving from home was never an option, even though she might have independent means. However, unmarried sons also appeared reluctant to leave the security of home life.

The family was a considerable cohesive force in the nineteenth century. Elderly parents would be cared for in the home, as can be seen from the grandmothers and grandfathers living in the various houses. Nieces and nephews would also be 'adopted', perhaps when a sister or brother was struggling to bring up a large family on a much smaller income.

Perhaps the most flamboyant resident of the square was Edward William Godwin. Born in Bristol in 1833, the son of a prosperous currier and leather cutter, he lived at No. 21 with his wife in the 1860s. He was educated in London at the Exton School in Highbury and, on his return to Bristol, was articled to William Armstrong, City Surveyor, Architect and Civil Engineer – with the emphasis very much on the 'engineer'. So little was known of architecture in this office that Godwin was largely self-taught and became responsible for the architectural commissions undertaken by the office at an unusually early age.

Indignant at the lack of recognition paid to his part in this work, in 1854, at the age of twenty-one, he set up his own practice and after a slow start, in 1861, won the competition for the design for Northampton Town Hall. He soon acquired other commissions; helping to restore St. Mary Redcliffe, the designs for Congleton Town Hall, Dromore Castle, Glenbegh Towers and additions to Castle Ashby. His early designs were in the neo-Gothic style with all the furniture and fittings designed to match.

For many years he had shown a marked preference for Japanese design, especially in his own surroundings, and this was particularly noticeable in his house in Portland Square. Godwin started designing furniture for the same reason as William Morris. His own words are almost an echo of Morris' nearly ten years earlier

> 'When I came to furniture I found that hardly anything could be bought ready-made that was at all suitable to the requirements of the case. I therefore set to work and designed a lot of furniture and, with a desire for economy, directed it to be made of deal ebonised'.

His love of all things Japanese spilled over into pattern designing which caused one critic to remark of a wallpaper design, 'Mr. Godwin has gone beyond most people's notions of the boundaries of civilisation and has added Japan'. The style of furniture which he designed for Dromore Castle and his own use emphasised this taste and the phrase Anglo-Japanese style was coined to describe it.

Godwin sold his designs for furniture to numerous companies, his wallpaper designs were made by Jeffrey and Co. and fabrics by Warner

& Ramm and J.W. & C. Ward. He also designed metalwork and tiles, wrote articles on Japanese culture, Saxon and Celtic architecture and contemporary issues in the architectural press.

By the late 1860s he had become friendly with Oscar Wilde, who was probably his most famous client, and also with James McNeill Whistler, the painter. In the last ten years of his life, Godwin designed some of his most revolutionary buildings, the White House in Chelsea for Whistler and a new entrance for the Fine Art Society. In 1881 he designed the entrance to, and redecorated the gallery for, Whistler's sensational exhibition of Venice pastels.

In 1862 he made the acquaintance of Ellen Terry, then aged fourteen years, who was to become one of the most famous actresses of the Victorian Theatre. She had come to Bristol with her elder sister, Kate, and both sisters were acting at the Prince's Theatre in Park Row (later destroyed by fire in World War II). Although Godwin's wife was delicate, the couple were very hospitable and as this excerpt from Ellen Terry's autobiography reveals, their gatherings made a great impression on a young actress:

> 'While my stage education was progressing apace, I was, through the influence of a very wonderful family whose acquaintance we made, having my eyes opened to beautiful things in art and literature. Mr. Godwin, the architect and archaeologist, was living in Bristol when Kate and I were at the Theatre Royal, and we used to go to his house for some of the Shakespeare readings in which our Bristol friends asked us to take part. This house, with its Persian rugs, beautiful furniture, its organ, its sense of design in every detail was a revelation to me, and the talk of its master and mistress made me think'.

In 1863 Ellen Terry appeared at the Theatre Royal, Bath, as Titania in *A Midsummer Night's Dream* and Godwin designed her dress. She writes again:

> 'Mr. Godwin designed my dress and we made it at his house in Bristol. He showed me how to damp it and "wring" it while it was wet, tying up the material as the Orientals do in their "tie and dry" process, so that, when it was dry and untied, it was all crinkled and clinging. This was the first lovely dress that I ever wore and I learned a great deal from it'.

Edward Godwin was secretary of the Bristol Shakespeare Society and because of his wife's ill health would visit the theatre by himself, particularly on benefit nights. It was on one of these occasions that the sisters were invited to a 'Shakespeare Reading' at the Godwin's house. Ellen Terry was a young girl at this time, but a mutual interest in the theatre and a love of the exotic had given their friendship an added dimension.

Ellen Terry remained in Bristol for almost two years. In 1863, at the age of sixteen years, she married the artist, George Watts; he was forty-six years old. Needless to say, the marriage lasted only a few months. Several years after her divorce and the death of Godwin's wife, the friends met again and this time their relationship blossomed. They set up home together in London and, although they never married, had two children, Edith, born in 1869 and Edward Gordon in 1872. Because the children were illegitimate it was inappropriate for them, in their circumstances, to be given the surname of either parent, and so a suitable name had to be found.

The parents' choice of surname was quite whimsical. On holiday in Scotland, the family happened upon the rock of Ailsa Craig. The couple were so taken with its beauty that the children were immediately given the name of Craig. Edward Gordon Craig was to become a famous theatrical designer, actor and director, whose non-realistic scenic design was to greatly influence theatre in Europe and the USA.

After the relationship with Edward Godwin ended in 1875, Ellen Terry was to remarry twice and Godwin married one of his students, named Beatrice. When Godwin died in 1886, Beatrice married James Whistler, but Ellen Terry never forgot her former lover. In later years she often spoke of 'the friends of those happy days in Bristol'.

One family whose name lived on into the twentieth century was that of Matthew Weir. In 1868 Matthew, a widower, was living at No. 1 with his three children aged twelve to fifteen years. He employed a housekeeper and a domestic servant. He was a draper and, living in the house were two drapers' assistants. Also living with them was John Weir, possibly his brother. The two men set up a drapery business in the name of M. & J. Weir.

In 1881 Matthew and John, together with Matthew's youngest son, Norman, were still at No. 1, but between 1885 and 1891 they had moved into Cumberland Street on the far side of Brunswick Square. In 1937 although the firm was still trading under the name of M. & J. Weir, none of that family was alive and the business had been acquired by a Mr. Brewer.

The family home had become a shop but Mr. Brewer was also a credit trader. He would call on customers on his bicycle, selling men's suits and other articles of clothing and household linen, taking from them between one and five shillings per week. As a suit could be purchased from around £2.00 the debt would soon be paid and Mr. Brewer would then encourage his customer to take on another purchase. This popular means of trading was the start of hire purchase and the credit card system we have to-day.

The years between 1811 and 1870 were happy times for those living in Portland Square. Undoubtedly, there would have been sadness and loss as well as joy and success, as happens in all communities, but the majority of residents must have presumed that their enviable lifestyle would continue for ever.

The decade between 1870 and 1880, however, was to see a fundamental change in the fortunes of this unique and elegant square.

Open fields beyond Brunswick Square, 1789.
From Barrett's *The History and Antiquities of the City of Bristol*

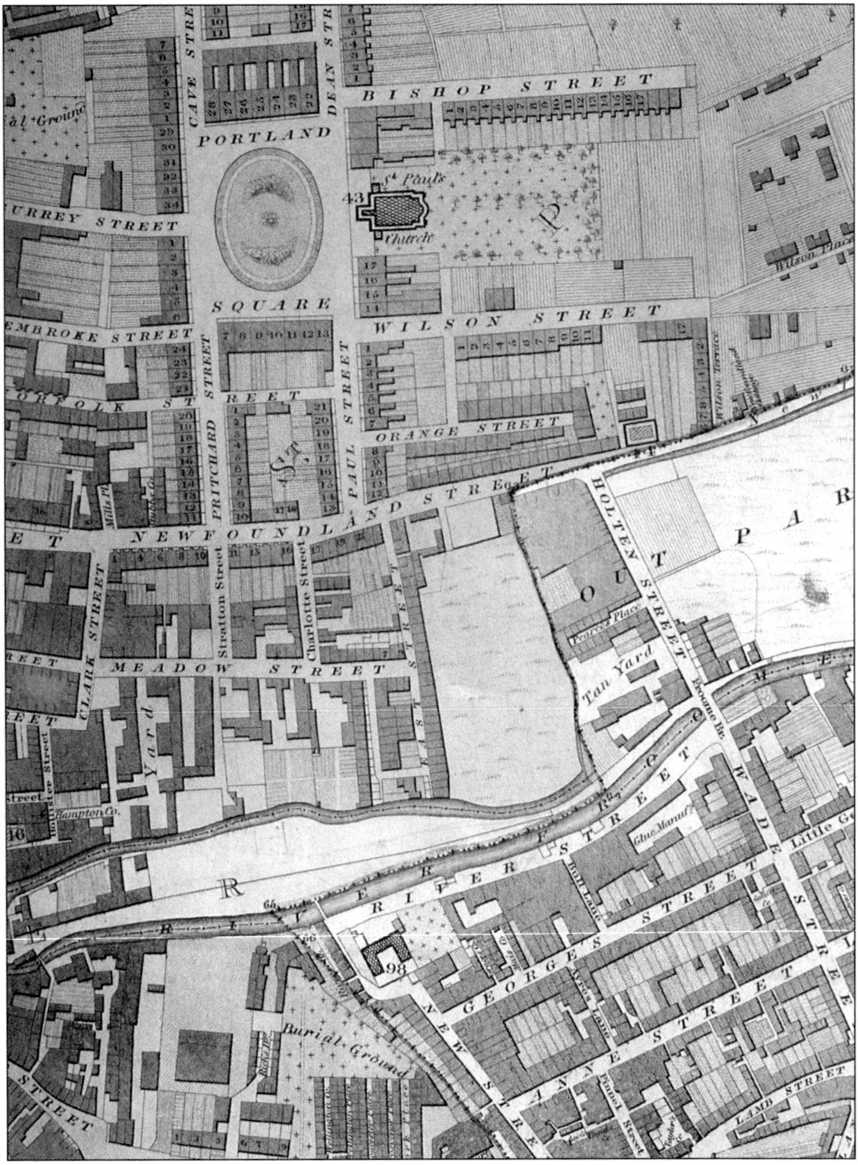

The Square laid out, 1828

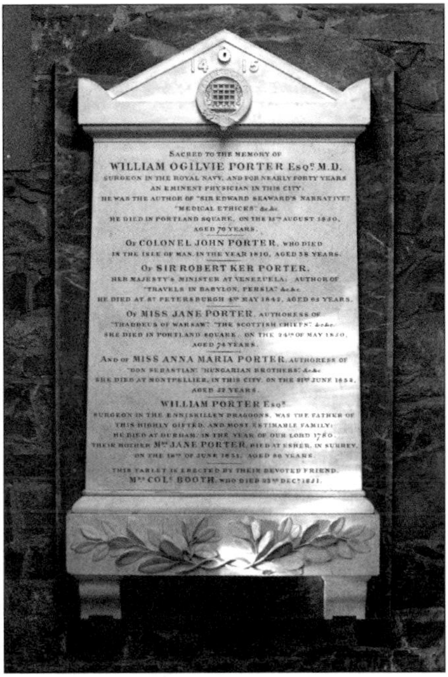

Memorial to William Ogilvie Porter and his family, in Bristol Cathedral

Tomb of Levi Ames in the graveyard behind the Unitarian Church. As Mayor of Bristol he was present at the ceremony to lay the foundation stone for St Paul's Church, April 23 1789

The Day Memorial in the Church of Saints Peter and Joseph

Ellen Terry, after a painting by her husband George Watts RA

The Excelsior Shoe Company. Production continued in the Square until 1966

G.F. Hutchings of the Excelsior Shoe Company

The fire at A.W. Smith's upholsterers' warehouse, No. 15 Portland Square, 28 April 1930. The firm subsequently moved to No. 8. *Courtesy Dennis Hill*

John Mardon's patented corrugating machine caused this fire at the English Corrugated Paper Co. at No 25 Portland Square, 26 October 1931.
Production continues under Christopher Mardon at the factory in Wilson Street.
Courtesy Dennis Hill

Kenneth James Mardon, grandfather of current MD Christopher Mardon, and head of the English English Corrugated Paper Co. at the time of the 1931 fire

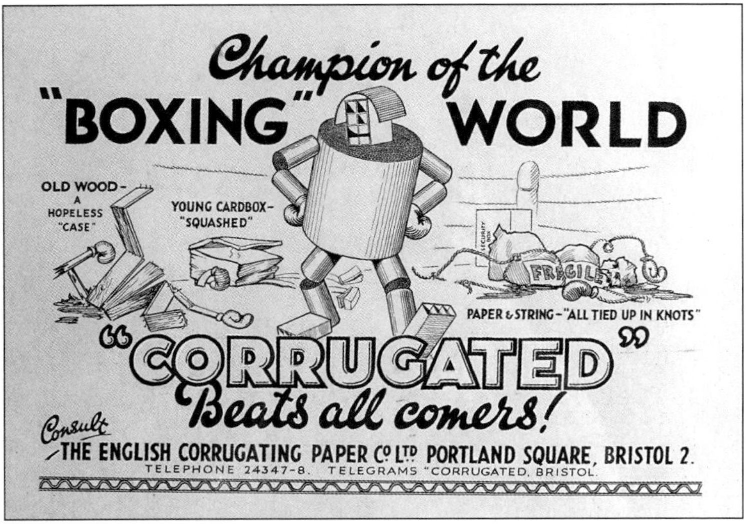

Advertisement for the English Corrugated Paper Co.

The Salvation Army Hostel on Pritchard Street

Edward Godwin

December 1940: Dean Street is virtually destroyed and St Paul's badly damaged by enemy bombs

The clockface of St Paul's is dedicated to the fallen of two World Wars

The wedding of Irene Elliot and Anthony Michael Clapp, 13 October 1962

The last wedding in the Square: Edna Elliot and Roger Hooper, 1 October 1966

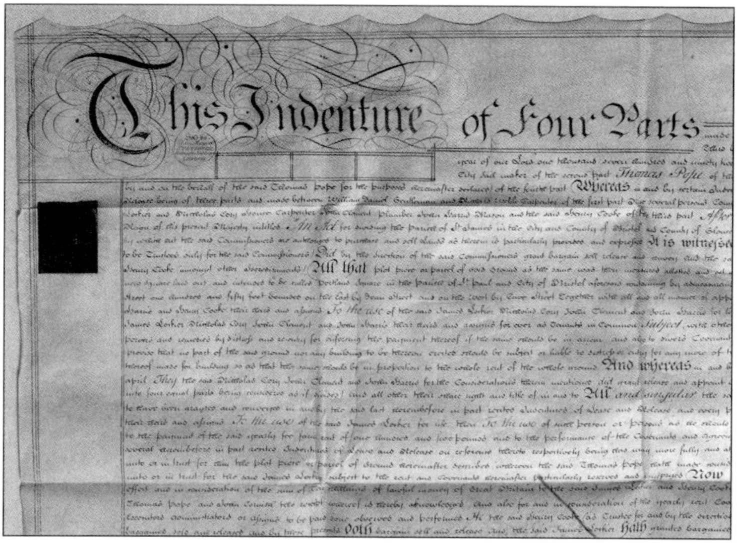

No. 27: the 1792 indenture of purchase

No. 27 restored as the Pierian Centre, 2002

Restoring St Paul's for Circomedia, 2003

The St Paul's restoration nearing completion, 2004

CHAPTER THREE

Flight

THE BRISTOL RIOTS OF 1831, CULMINATING IN THE ALMOST TOTAL destruction of Queen's Square, led to a transfer of prosperous Bristolians out of the city to the relative safety of a new suburb. This leafy paradise with spectacular views across the Avon Gorge was, of course, Clifton. Ambitious architects competed against each other in building what was to become one of the finest areas of Georgian architecture in the country. Their work was virtually completed by the latter part of the 1850s and the villas and town houses erected between the Victoria Rooms and Clifton Village were seized upon by all those who could afford them.

Why then did the residents of Portland Square not join in this exodus from the city for another two decades? Possibly the mere toppling of a statue was not seen as too threatening to their way of life and the square must still have retained an air of quiet gentility.

However, once a few families had left the remainder followed and, within the space of ten short years, what had once been considered the epitome of gracious living had become an 'inner city area'.

At the end of the nineteenth century Bristol had become England's leading city in the manufacture of boots and shoes and it was not long before almost every house in the Square had become a boot factory.

There were a few residents who remained faithful to their old homes. As we have seen Ann and Thomas Beddoe and Mrs. Wills remained in the square until their deaths and, of course, the vicars of St. Paul's church continued to use No. 18 until its closure. However, as we trace the residents' departure we can see a steady exodus of the gentry. They flocked to the elegant squares and terraces of Clifton as those before them had rushed to acquire property in Portland Square.

Perhaps by the 1870s the square was not quite what it had been fifty years before. As we have seen, Eliza Rootsey had turned No. 25 into a boarding house in 1857 and in 1861, William Lemmon, the owner of No.15, had taken in five boarders. This is always a sign of a declining environment, as were the proliferation of boarding schools as opposed to a single family with coach and horses and several servants. However, until the 1870s the square was still enjoying a fine respectability.

The first intimation that all was not well was the fact that, in the 1871 census, three houses were listed as uninhabited, Nos. 8, 9 and 12; the latter had been vacant since 1863. In previous years every house had had an occupant.

A number of families who had established businesses in the neighbourhood also remained in the square after 1880; Matthew Weir, the wholesale draper, at No. 1 and William Kearsey, the corn and flour merchant at No. 13.

There were also several widows who presumably owned their properties and were thus able to remain in these large houses. Matilda Robertson, a widow of independent means remained at No. 9 after the death of her husband, Samuel. She was fifty-three years old and had one daughter living at home. She took in four boarders and kept one domestic servant. She remained in the house until 1880.

Charles Baker, his wife Caroline, son Benjamin and daughter Harriett had lived at No. 21 for many years, certainly as far back as the late 1860s, although the actual date is difficult to ascertain. Charles seems to have had no profession, so we must assume that he belonged to the gentry. At his death, Caroline, together with her daughter took in two lodgers and also a nephew. According to the census, they were still there in 1891. Also as mentioned previously, there was Elizabeth Rootsey at No. 25 and Jane Dykes, widow of Henry, the railway official, with her three daughters at No. 31. The Nott family, also involved in the railways, remained in the square until the mid 1880s. Possibly the two families had become friendly and stayed as neighbours until Jane's death in 1885.

There were also a number of physicians and surgeons who still found the square sufficiently prestigious to remain. In 1861, a surgeon named Joseph Goodall Lansdown then aged fifty-six years had moved into No. 10. With him were his wife, Emily, and their six children aged between eight and twenty-four years, all unmarried. They kept a cook and two domestic servants. In the 1871 census, Joseph is listed as a widower. All his children were still at home. One daughter, aged thirty-two years, was married and lived in the house together with her son aged one year. Here again, it is impossible to uncover the circumstances of her situation. Also in the house was a nephew, who was a college undergraduate together with three domestic servants. The family had left by 1876.

In the 1881 census there were four members of the medical profession listed. Physician, George Rogers, lived at No. 6 with his wife, two unmarried daughters aged thirty and thirty-one years and one boarder, a retired banker aged seventy-eight years. They kept a coachman, a cook and a parlourmaid.

Surgeon William Hawkins, aged twenty-four years, was now head of the household at No. 16. Charles Newman was still at No. 19 and a General Practitioner named David Bain had moved into No. 32.

Some of the houses had taken on names; No. 6 was Arundel House, No. 4 was St. Clement's Vicarage, Nos. 7-12 were Portland House, No. 16 was Windsor House and No. 23, Woodstock House. However, the most unusual name in the square was given to No. 25. The name was Draper and was quite obviously unofficial.

No. 25, as previously mentioned, was bought by Samuel Henderson and the house remained in the possession of his family until 1902. His granddaughter, Mary Ludlow Henderson, who had inherited one half of the property, was married on the 18th August 1824 in St. James' Church to Richard Short. Unfortunately, her husband died the following year. The deeds give no indication of the cause of his death, only that he was buried in the Unitarian Burial Ground of Brunswick Square. Mary then married Thomas Spilsbury, however the date of their marriage is unknown. Mary's only child, the son of Richard Short, was named Richard Samuel Henderson Spilsbury Short.

Richard was married on the 8th August 1850 at the Hope Chapel, Clifton and he and his wife, Ann, received half of the rents and profits of No. 25. The house had been leased since 1879, at an annual rent of £80.00, to a firm of drapers, Jones & Co., who had a large store in the centre of Bristol. The store was called 'Jones & Co.' and was originally located in Wine Street, but was bombed during the Second World War. After the war a new store was built on the site which is now occupied by Debenhams in Broadmead. The change over took place in the early 1960s when Jones & Co. finally ceased trading.

The firm used No. 25, presumably both the house and coachhouse as lodgings for their staff. In 1881 there were twenty-four draper's assistants and three domestic servants all living on the premises and in 1891 their numbers had increased to thirty-seven draper's assistants, three cashiers and three domestics. The house was run by a matron who, no doubt, introduced a rigid set of rules.

There had always been merchants and artisans in the square and in the 1880s this trend continued. A wheelwright named William Venman moved into No. 2 in 1874. He and his wife, Mary Anne, had seven children, four sons and three daughters. In 1881 the children were all unmarried and living at home. The eldest daughter, Marianne, aged twenty-three years was in charge of household duties, while Arthur aged twenty-one years was listed as a painter. It is unclear whether he was a house painter or a fine artist. Ellen, aged nineteen years, was a teacher and Florence, aged eighteen years was apprenticed to a stationer. George and Frank, aged seventeen and fifteen years were apprenticed to a draper and grocer respectively. The youngest son, Alfred, aged nine years was still a scholar. The family kept one domestic servant.

In 1873, Thomas Clements, gentleman, and his wife left No. 3 and the house was taken over by wholesale boot manufacturers, Hutchings & King. However, their business did not last and in 1880 a wholesale grocer named John Iles took possession. In the census of 1881 he is recorded as being forty-five years of age and his wife, Mary, was forty-one. They had one unmarried daughter, Clara aged twenty-two years living at home. They also had three sons, Charles, Thomas and Robert, aged five years, three years and three weeks. The records do not show whether Mary was mother to all four children. The family employed two nurses, a cook and a housemaid.

After their departure in 1885, Dr. Gorham Whitcombe Grote, LRCP, took over the house. Unfortunately, as he was only in residence for five years and had left before the 1891 census, there is no record of any family or servants he may have had.

In 1876, a publisher named William Mackenzie moved into No. 5 and his agent John Baker shared the house. By 1881, John Baker, now aged fifty-one years was in sole possession together with his wife and six children. Their ages ranged between twenty-four and seven years and they kept no domestic servants. There are no occupations for the children listed in the census but all were unmarried.

One house whose history has not been examined is No. 23. The original occupier was Thomas Castle but the records give only his name. In 1822 an oil importer, John Hare junior, who had been an active supporter of William Wilberforce's work for the abolition of slavery, took up residence and in 1835 a minister, Rev. Samuel Summers, was the occupier.

There is far more information in the census of 1851. The house was leased to James Ball, aged sixty-five years, a retired maltster and hop factor. The name of his firm was J.T. & W.W. Ball and the business was at No. 2 Wilder Street. His wife, Amelia, was sixty years old and they had five children. There were three unmarried daughters aged thirty-nine, thirty-two and twenty-four years, a son aged thirty-six who was a malster (presumably in the family business) and their youngest son, aged twenty-one, who was a wine merchant. Also in the house was a female lodger with her two daughters, aged six and one year. They employed four domestic servants.

In 1861 there was another family living in the house. Robert Morris was a timber merchant and came from Somerset. He was fifty-eight years old and his wife, Sybil, was forty-two, between them they had eight children. The eldest, a son aged fourteen years, was a bank clerk. The others ranged from one to thirteen years. There was also a boarder, a fifteen year old student. This family kept two domestic servants.

By 1863 the family had left and the house was taken over by a surgeon named Robert Fendick. He was the Registrar of births and deaths for the St. Paul's district. Also living at No. 23 was George Fendick. He, too, was a surgeon but the records do not show the relationship between the two men, presumably they were brothers.

In 1881 a draper named George Grierson took up residence. He was thirty-two years old, the same age as his wife. They had four children aged nine months to four years and employed a nursemaid, a domestic servant and a groom. Also lodging in the house were two drapers and there were also two visiting drapers. Mr Grierson was possibly conducting his drapery business from home and it was about this time that the square changed from a purely residential to a mixed residential and commercial area. However, this was to change radically as we shall see in the early part of the next century, when the square was to become almost completely industrialised.

As the houses fell vacant and very few people chose to live in the square, they were quickly snapped up by firms who employed a small workforce. It was realised that the rooms on the ground and first floors were large and airy and could easily be modified for the production of small items.

The domination of the boot and shoe sector did not take place overnight and in the 1890s there was an interesting mix of establishments. There were, unfortunately, many empty houses in the square and in the 1891 census at least ten uninhabited properties were recorded.

Although the remainder were by now in commercial or industrial use, there were still families in residence. A provision merchant named Benjamin Callcott had moved into No. 2 with his life, Louisa, and three children. There was a daughter aged nine years, a son aged six years and a baby of seven days. Also in the house was the sister of Louisa who was a certified nurse, together with a domestic servant.

Another provision merchant and dealer in groceries, William Hall, lived at No. 3 with his wife, Elizabeth, a daughter aged twenty-three years and a son of twenty-two who was a clerk in the provision warehouse. They kept two domestic servants.

At No. 4 was George Laws who was a Clerk in Holy Orders. He came from London and brought his wife Ellen, two daughters aged four years and ten months and two domestic servants. No. 5 was still occupied by the book publisher, John Baker and his wife, Marion. However, there were no children recorded as living at home at that time.

An insurance agent named Samuel Jordan from Gloucester had come to live at No. 6. His wife was Sarah and they had eight children, six daughters and two sons. The oldest daughter, Amy, was a music teacher and the second, Bertha, was an assistant teacher. The eldest son, Samuel, was a booking clerk and the third daughter, Nelly, an insurance clerk. The fourth daughter, Florence, was a pupil teacher and the remaining three children were listed as scholars. There is no record of any domestic servants.

No. 18 was, of course, still occupied by the vicar of St. Paul's and in 1891 the Rev. James Davidson, B.A. was the incumbent. He was a widower and lived with his son, who was a student of theology, a niece, a granddaughter and a lodger of independent means. There was one domestic servant. Unfortunately, the records to not reveal the intricacies of this family history.

A woollen merchant from Scotland, Angus MacKenzie, had come to live at No. 20 with his wife, Alice, and their five young children. They were aged between three and fourteen years and the family kept no domestic servants.

The square at this time was still a lively residential area and there must have been a considerable amount of socialising in the evenings and at weekends. Although, as we shall see, production of various types of clothing and other businesses were encroaching upon the lives of the residents, these operations were probably fairly unobtrusive, at least until the turn of the century.

In 1880 a box manufacturer, named Charles Coomer, had come to live at No. 26 with his wife and five young children. They were aged between two and fourteen years and the family employed one domestic servant. It is not clear, however, whether the business was conducted from home.

A family named Pitts lived at No. 27 from 1856, when William Baker vacated the property, until 1871. William Alfred Pitts was a public accountant and auctioneer. His wife was Rachel and they had five children. Living with them was Jane Smith, William's mother-in-law, aged seventy-four years and a niece, Catherine Stanton, aged fourteen years. The family employed a groom and a domestic servant. After the Pitts family left No. 27 in 1871, the house was occupied by a lace manufacturer named Henry Makepeace together with his wife and two children. In 1876 there was a change of tenant and the house became a factory, run by Pearce Bros., making hats and caps. The firm remained there until 1915.

One of the first residents of the square to operate his business from home was a wholesale tea dealer from Scotland, William Thompson. He came to live at No. 28 in 1861 and his opening hours were advertised as being from 8-10 a.m. He remained there until 1880 when a firm of tea dealers, Gane & Poole, moved into the house. They had possibly bought his business and remained in the house for five years. In 1885 they transferred their operations to No. 31 and remained at that address until 1905, when the business was taken over by Wm. Thomson & Co.

The firm that moved into No. 28 in 1885 manufactured stays or corsets. They were the Williams brothers and worked from that address until 1905. Prewett & Co. were also stay manufacturers at No. 9 from 1880 to 1885. The largest corset manufacturers in the square, Young & Neilson, moved into two premises in 1880. These were Nos. 11 and 12 and the firm was obviously very successful as they remained in the square until 1930.

It was, however, the manufacture of boots and shoes which was predominant in the square. Boots were in great demand in the Bristol and Somerset coal fields and the industrial areas of South Wales and Ireland and Bristol boot and shoe firms employed thousands of workers.

The first wholesale boot manufacturer in Portland Square was Robert G. Whiting, who began his business at No. 7 in 1872, the house having been empty for four years. He was joined, in 1876, by a man named Webb and the firm Whiting & Webb quickly flourished. By 1880 they had enlarged their business to incorporate No. 8, which was also vacant, and in 1885 took over No. 9 when Prewett & Co. moved out. The firm remained in business until 1891.

Another successful firm of shoe manufacturers was Hutchins & May. They began with one house, No. 22, in 1880 and when the Grierson family left No. 23, expanded next door. A boot manufacturer named

Edmund Quick was in operation for a short while, from 1880 to 1885, at No. 24. After his departure the house remained empty for a few years before the inevitable happened and Hutchins & May expanded yet again. The firm remained in business until 1913.

Nos. 32 and 33 were also in the shoe business. The firm of R.W. Ashley, shoe manufacturers, were installed in 1880 and by 1913 had taken over No. 31. The firm remained in business until 1923.

Such a large boot and shoe industry necessitated an efficient delivery of materials and in 1885 a leather merchant, John C. Ford, moved into No. 16. He remained there until 1891 when the house became vacant. It remained empty until 1905 when it was occupied by yet another boot manufacturer, George Nash & Sons. This firm survived two World Wars and remained in the square until 1972.

Perhaps the most forward looking of all the boot manufacturers in the square at that time was the firm of Pope & Co. John Pope came from Crediton in Devon and moved into No. 14 in 1891. With him was his wife and two sons who were also in the business. There was also a son aged 6 years. John's parents, William and Mary, and his sister-in-law, Margaret Harriers, also lived in the house. They kept two domestic servants.

John Pope was determined to modernise his business and in 1894 he constructed, at the rear of his house, an impressive four-storey, red-brick extension. The whole building was then used as a factory. Portland Square had finally become an industrial area.

As the century drew to its close, it became clear that Portland Square could no longer maintain its status as a desirable residential area. The industrialisation, together with its position in the centre of the city and the deterioration of the surrounding district had conspired to transform this once elegant square into a shabby and unappreciated corner of Bristol.

CHAPTER FOUR

A New Century

THE TWENTIETH CENTURY WAS TO WITNESS A SIGNIFICANT CHANGE in Bristol's role as a port and 'Gateway to the West'. As ships grew larger and could no longer be accommodated in the narrow Avon Gorge, Bristol lost its status as England's second city. Always innovative in the field of transport, the *s.s. Great Britain* being restored to its former glory, Bristol turned its gaze to the skies and built the mighty giants of the air, the Brabazon and Corcorde.

Portland Square, however, still had its feet firmly on the ground with the manufacture of boots and shoes; although this particular area of manufacture was to steadily decline as the century progressed.

The established shoe manufacturers were fortunate in being able to remain in business for a number of years. Most noticeable among these were the firms of R.W. Ashley, John Pope & Co. and Hutchins & May.

There were other firms who entered the square after the turn of the century, some of whom shared the large houses with unrelated trades. In 1905 J. Flook & Sons, shoe manufacturers moved into No. 10. In 1927, when perhaps their business was struggling, they sublet a part of the building to a draper named Henry Baker. By 1944, two furniture manufacturers, W. Rookledge and the Cavendish Furniture Co., were also subletting.

In 1907, No.15 was home to Chittock & Co., boot and shoe manufacturers, a commercial agent named John T. King, together with G. Richardson & Co., leather merchants. The latter firm had gone by 1910.

Another extremely successful boot manufacturer was the firm of George Nash & Sons. They had set up their factory at No. 16 in 1905 and in 1913, when No. 15 became vacant, moved next door. In 1915 a firm of wholesale clothiers, W.A. Hicks & Co. joined them in both houses. By 1923 it seems as though George Nash had consolidated his factory into No. 16. W.A. Hicks had left No. 15 and in his place was a firm of wholesale bedding and bedstead manufacturers, H.H. Hill, together with an upholsterers' warehouseman, A.W. Smith. In 1931 Smith moved to Wilson Street and Hill moved to No. 8. George Nash, however, remained at No. 16 until 1972.

There were several other boot manufacturers and leather factors in the square at that time. The Eglington boot factory at No. 29 between 1905 and 1938, Walter S. Betty, a boot factor at No. 13 from 1905 until 1920 and at No. 21 a boot and leather merchant named C.S. Harris. He was at this address from 1905 until 1910. There was also a factory at No. 3, run by Headford & Erwin who were trading from 1905 until 1923.

Just as it seemed as though this trade was coming to an end in Portland Square, a new firm arrived and breathed new life into the industry. The firm was G.F. Hutchings & Co. Ltd. and was known as the Excelsior Shoe Company.

In 1923 they moved into Nos. 1, 3 and 4 but it was not until 1933 that they were able to expand into No. 2. This house had served as a practice for two doctors, John Longley, M.B. and John Joseph Powell, M.D. from 1905. G.F. Hutchings, who was possibly related to the boot manufacturers Hutchings & King, built a factory behind these four houses but it is not possible to verify the date of this building. Was it 1923 or 1933? Perhaps the doctors were happy to have a factory behind their house. It would possibly have increased their practice, patients, of course, having to pay for doctors' services at that time. The Excelsior Shoe Company remained in the square until 1966.

As the boot and shoe industry declined, so other industries became prominent. In 1913, a firm of book binders and gold blockers named

W.H. Mogridge & Co. moved into No. 1 Portland Square. By 1923 the firm had become Roberts Bros. & Mogridge. Perhaps to make way for the Excelsior Shoe Company, or perhaps because they, too, wished to expand, the company transferred their operations into Nos. 32, 33 and 34. They remained there until 1944 when they re-located to Pritchard Street.

The furniture industry featured quite strongly in the square. Apart from the two firms at No. 10, W. Rookledge and the Cavendish Furniture Co., a firm of cabinet makers named P.E. Gane were situated at Nos. 22 and 26. This firm was well established, also having a shop in Park Street, and occupied the two houses from 1913 until 1940.

In 1938, wholesale cabinet makers, Joseph Whiting & Son, moved into Nos. 11 and 12. There were also two firms of upholsterers, G.J. Millman & Sons at No. 7, who were there from 1930 to 1938 and at No. 15, the aforementioned upholsterers' warehouseman, A.W. Smith. The firm of H.H. Hill who moved from No. 15 to No. 8 in 1931 remained in these premises until 1960 sharing the house from 1950 with a firm of hardware factors, Plasgoods, Ltd.

One of the more successful firms in the square was the English Corrugating Paper Company, Ltd. The origins of the firm date from 1820 with James Mardon of Mardon, Son & Hall, paper and card manufacturers. James's two sons, Heber and John, who were half brothers, married two daughters of Mr. Hall. In 1907, the firm sold out to the Imperial Tobacco Co. and John Mardon left to set up the English Corrugating Paper Company. He had patented a machine for making corrugated paper and in 1908 moved into No. 28 Portland Square. Over the years the business expanded into No. 27 and in 1927 the paper making machines were installed in No. 25.

The great grandson of the original owner, Christopher Mardon, tells a heartwarming story of old loyalties. In 1931, an employee was working at one of the machines, which was fired by gas. Suddenly, one of the sheets of paper caught fire and instinctively he threw the burning paper over his shoulder. Unfortunately, it landed near some rolls of cardboard and in an instant the room was ablaze. Before the fire brigade could put out the flames, the entire house was gutted.

The firm was insured with the Guardian Royal Exchange but when Kenneth James Mardon, who was then head of the firm, inspected the policy he found that it had lapsed a short while prior to the fire. Contrary to expectations, the insurance company honoured its commitment and, according to Christopher Mardon, English Corrugating remained with the Guardian Royal until his grandfather's death in 1973. The money from the insurance enabled the company to rebuild No. 25 and business continued until World War II when, unfortunately, the building, together with Nos. 22, 23, 24 and 25, was destroyed in the bombing raids, as were Nos. 29, 30 and 31.

In the early part of the century, and in fact continuing to the present day, there was a proliferation of services in the square which reflected both its geographical location in the centre of the city and its 'inner city' aspect.

An interesting development in the square in 1905 was the opening of a restaurant at No. 20 which was extended to No. 21 in 1910. The owner was Mr. F.J. Hall but there is no record of the nature of the restaurant, whether it served breakfast, lunchtime or evening meals.

In 1915, No.27 became the headquarters of the Bristol Boy Scouts and a shop was opened on the ground floor, selling both scouts and guides uniforms. In 1933 the English Corrugating Paper Co. moved in but for a few short years between 1946 and 1952 the boy scouts were once again in residence.

Peter Barnfield, whose father ran the shop at that time, tells of the many fires he witnessed in the square as a young lad. He lived in the coach house at the rear of the building but each time he heard the fire engines he would watch from the front windows. He could recall at least nine fires, one of which was in No. 27 itself. Major Morstadt, the Scouts Commissioner, lived on the top floor of the house and one night his chimney caught fire, much to the delight of the young Peter, who could watch the fire fighters at close range.

For many years, the Salvation Army, played an important role in the square. In July 1916 a Hostel for Women was opened at No. 21, to be supervised by a committee formed for that purpose and worked by the Salvation Army. An imposing ceremony took place in the St. Paul's Parish Room, attended by many dignitaries; the Lord Mayor, the Bishops of Clifton and Bristol, together with Sir Frank Wills as the chairman of the committee.

Sir Frank outlined the scheme and explained that the city had originally intended to provide a Municipal Women's Hostel. That project had been prevented by the war, yet it was felt that something must be done to provide lodgings for those women 'whose greatest crime was lack of means'. A small Home for this purpose had been established in Brigstocke Road but it was handicapped through lack of funds.

The new committee would finance and equip the larger premises in the square and generous gifts had already been received in money and kind. About £80.00 more was required towards initial expenses and yearly subscriptions would also be needed.

The Duchess of Beaufort had consented to open the Hostel and declared that it was a work demanding the sympathy not only of women but of everyone in the city and the Empire. There was a tremendous migration of women, due to the break-up of the home, which had never been known in England before and there was a need for the highest national and civic patriotism to deal with the problems that would arise.

The Hostel had fifteen rooms with three grades of accommodation for women – twopence, fourpence and sixpence being the charges for lodging, with correspondingly small charges for food.

The bedrooms were mostly arranged on the cubicle system, with curtains forming the divisions. There were bathrooms on most of the floors and plenty of wash basins; there was also a washhouse available for the use of inmates.

In the basement, beds were kept in readiness for any late arrivals or cases needing special attention, and for these there was a separate entrance, so that the upper part of the house would not be disturbed.

The resident officer in charge was Adjutant Gardner, acting as Assistant Warden to Lieut-Colonel Goldsmith. They had previously been running the Brigstocke Road Hostel.

In 1926 a report put the price of beds at sixpence, eightpence and tenpence. Odd meals or full board were provided and there was a reduction to those who paid in advance. At that time the Hostel accommodated thirty-six women, a few being old-age pensioners. The oldest inmate was ninety-two years old, the youngest was thirteen. This girl slept at the Hostel because there was no bedroom for her in her own overcrowded home.

After the closure of the Hostel in 1936, No. 21 became a Vocational Training School until it, too, was destroyed by bombs in World War II.

The Salvation Army had a Men's Hostel at Nos. 7 and 8, which was acquired when the Milk Street Hostel was burned down in 1939. It was meant to be a temporary measure but the war intervened. It was not closed until 1975 when the present Men's Hostel in Little George Street was opened. The Hostel in the square had one hundred and forty-seven cubicles and dormitories.

There were other institutions in the square at this time, set up to support the men and women who had come to Bristol looking for work. In 1891, the St. Paul's Mission House was opened at No. 30 and in 1905 the Y.W.C.A. opened their doors at No. 17. It remained in operation until 1914 when the Mission House transferred to that address.

The years between the two World Wars were fairly stable for those working in the square. A number of businesses did come and go but the church continued to hold services and the Great Depression did not seem to affect the production and sale of goods for the majority of firms located there.

However, World War II brought much devastation and disruption to the square. On the 2nd December, 1940 there was a bombing raid in St. Paul's and Dean Street took a direct hit. Forty-four people were killed in that street and also in the warden's post situated at No. 22 Portland Square. Dean Street was entirely demolished as were Nos. 21 to 25. The church also suffered bomb damage. In a subsequent raid Nos. 29 and 30 were also demolished.

The armistice in 1945, coinciding with the end of the first half of the twentieth century, marked the lowest ebb in the fortunes of this remarkable square.

During the war, the iron railings, so important in defining the houses and garden, were removed for the war effort and the garden itself was left to become a wilderness. All this, together with the bombed and disfigured buildings must have reduced Portland Square to a total antithesis of its original splendour. And so it remained for a number of years, licking its wounds and hoping for better things to come.

CHAPTER FIVE

Stirrings

AFTER THE WAR IN 1945, BRITAIN, LIKE THE REST OF EUROPE, struggled to come to terms with the end of hostilities. The returning soldiers needed jobs and so the women, who had filled the ammunition factories and ploughed the land, were tempted back into their homes with promises of new cookers and longer hemlines.

Portland Square also languished for a number of years but plans were being laid to rebuild and restore the bombed and damaged buildings.

In 1947 The English Corrugating Paper Co. Ltd. sold the plot of land on which No. 25 had stood to the cabinet makers Joseph Whiting & Son. Frank, the son, was now head of the firm and he also acquired the land relating to Nos. 22 to 24. Included in the sale of the land was the right to any money owing for war damage.

After the fire in 1933, No. 25 had been rebuilt to the same specifications as its original Georgian structure, namely a house at the front and stables or outbuildings at the rear. With the complete demolition of this area, Frank Whiting decided to build a modern factory behind the original facade, which had not been destroyed. He designed an open plan building on four floors, excluding the basement, stretching from the square in the front through to Chapter Street.

The whole building was strengthened with RSJ beams across each floor 10'6" apart and the work was completed in 1950. So well was No. 25 constructed that there was no money left for the remaining three houses.

In 1962 Frank Whiting sold No. 25 to a carpet wholesaler, A.V. Humphries and with the money from this sale he built himself a single-storey factory on the remaining land. He stayed in Portland

Square until 1971 when he sold the property and moved his operation to Keynsham.

During the two decades of the 1950s and 1960s the square, apart from the rebuilding of No. 25, retained its rather forlorn appearance. The Salvation Army Hostel was in need of a face lift. As there was no public money at that time for the cleaning of the stonework, which was an expensive procedure, the facades of the buildings remained grimy and pitted from bomb damage.

The square continued as a light industrial area, with the Excelsior Shoe factory at Nos. 1-4, George Nash's boot factory at No. 16 and the Victoria Flour Co. at No. 6. A furniture manufacturer, W.A. Davies, occupied No. 13 between 1968 and 1973. The Singer Sewing Machine Co. Ltd. used No. 26 as a servicing station for their machines and were in the square from 1956 until 1972.

A wholesale chemist, Ferris & Co. Ltd., had moved into Nos. 31-34 in 1944 and remained there until 1960 when another wholesale chemist, J.R. Gibb, took over the premises. The English Corrugating Paper Co. Ltd. remained at No. 27 until 2001.

The square was also home to a number of firms in the printing and graphics sector. Graphic Engravers Ltd. occupied No. 14 from 1956 to 1962. They were part of the Burleigh Press Group which was owned by the Corrigan family and was the largest firm of printers in Bristol.

The Cabot Press, at No. 5, had withstood the bombing and operated in the square from 1938 until 1969; the printers Knight & Sherborne were at No. 15 from 1950 to 1958 and at No. 21 the lithographic plate makers, B.E.S. Technical Press Ltd. shared the building with advertising agents, the Clifton Studios.

Tom Newick & Co. (Bristol) Ltd, who were hardware factors, had occupied Nos. 23 and 24 from 1923 until the houses were bombed. They relocated to No. 20 and remained there until 1972 when they moved their operation to No. 19. There they joined the wholesale clothing firm, Segar & Co.

Many of the properties during these two decades housed multiple businesses and services. Between 1950 and 1969 there were six such concerns at No. 9; the British Legion (Bristol County Headquarters); a wholesale jeweller, named V. Schlesinger who also had a shop in Fairfax Street; the City of Bristol Ex-Services Club; Permanoid Cable manufacturers; F.J. Ackland & Co. (accountants) and Morris-Baird Installations.

In 1964, No. 17 became the home of the National Union of Tailors and Garment Workers. They shared the house with the Etna Lighting & Heating Co. until 1968 and then with a firm of general merchants, Dean & Harper.

The firm of J.M. Millett & Sons, sportswear retailers, used No. 15 as a warehouse for their goods from 1960 until 1969.

There were two substantial electrical wholesalers in the square at this time. Curwen Miller & Co. Ltd. were at No. 12 from 1958 and in 1966 the firm of Denmans moved into Nos. 1-4, left vacant by the Excelsior Shoe Co. They remained in the square until 1973.

The 1970s were a turning point in the fortunes of Portland Square. As the silicon chip industry moved west, prestigious firms discovered the benefits of an 'architectural gem' which was linked to London by rail and the M4. Bristol airport served Paris, Amsterdam and Dublin and within a number of years the M32 was to link the motorway directly with the square.

The *Evening Post* was keeping an eye on the exciting developments in the square. In a number of articles it reported on specific companies who were moving in for various reasons.

One such article, written by Max Barnes on Tuesday, 8th August 1972, stated that planning permission had been received to go ahead with an office block on the site of Nos. 22-24 Portland Square. The facade was to be built of freestone to match the exact Georgian details of the original design. Mr. Clive Lilley, the Managing Director of the firm of property developers, stated that 'this is just part of the city's plan to restore the square completely which, when completed, will be one of the most beautiful in Bristol or any city'.

Environmentalists had, at last, won the battle to restore the character of the city in its grandest days and the Council had designated Brunswick and Portland Squares, together with Cumberland Street and Cave Street, as a conservation area. After three years this was upgraded to an area of outstanding status and that made it possible to obtain grants to restore the building.

In a further article in 1975, James Belsey interviewed the Managing Director of a firm making and marketing data processing equipment. Jimmy James was the jet-setting executive of Image Data Products Ltd. and the company had just moved into Nos. 1-4 Portland Square.

Apparently, Mr. James had planned to set up shop in the Thames Valley. It was only at the eleventh hour, when he was shaving, the very morning he was due to sign the contract for a Thames Valley headquarters, that the story changed. On the radio he heard the director of a firm in the silicon chip industry explaining why he had chosen Bristol. Mr. James immediately contacted Bristol City Council and seven months later he moved into Portland Square.

He mentioned all the advantages but insisted that the square itself was the biggest success of all. 'Overseas visitors fall in love with it at once.' he explained. 'They see a beautiful Georgian square which is being renovated to the very highest standard. From the square it is an easy walk to so much history in central Bristol, from St. Mary Redcliffe to the Nails outside the Corn Exchange. They are all enchanted.'

Even though from his windows Mr. James could see the scaffolding around the former Salvation Army Hostel at Nos. 7 and 8, which was being gutted for further restoration, he was not to be daunted. He could see, from the gardens which had been transformed into one of the prettiest parks in the city, together with several of the buildings which had already been scrubbed clean and re-roofed, that he was on to a winner.

One important development in Bristol which directly impinged on the affairs of my family was the reconstruction of the St. James Barton complex.

My husband was born in Cumberland Street in 1923 and, at his birth, his father, whose name was Jack, decided to set up business on his own. He converted the front room of their home, No. 7, into a store room and called his new venture the Jay Bee Warehouse. Business was good and the stock gradually filled the downstairs rooms, climbed the stairs and threatened to engulf the bedrooms. Drastic action was called for and the family moved to the suburbs.

The warehouse remained at that address until 1970 when planning permission was given for the redevelopment of the St. James Barton complex. Unfortunately, this involved the demolition of No. 7 Cumberland Street and the Jay Bee Warehouse was obliged to relocate. The circumstances could not have been more favourable. No. 25 Portland Square was for sale and although the square at that time was still in a dilapidated condition, the building itself was perfect. A.V. Humphries, Ltd. who had become Humphries & Tapling (South & West) Ltd., were looking for premises away from the city centre and were anxious to sell and so the Jay Bee Warehouse found itself in an open-plan building, equipped with lift and loading bay.

This was very different from the cramped conditions of Cumberland Street, a family home converted into a warehouse. With no chance of stock control, the staff had to rely on memory which, fortunately for the customers, never failed them.

The Jay Bee did not need more than three floors for their operation and in 1972 the top two floors were let to an electronics firm, Digicon

Electronics Ltd. They manufactured computers and control mechanisms and needed quite a large area for their operation. The Singer Sewing Machine Co. in No. 26, also wishing to let their two top floors, agreed to have communicating doors constructed between the two buildings. Unfortunately, after five years Digicon went out of business and the floors were unoccupied for some years.

When local radio stations were given licences in the 1980s, many pirate stations were also set up to service the differing tastes of the listening public.

The pirate radio station ‘For the People’ (FTP) was set up in Bristol by a team of black broadcasters whose aim was to reach the 15-25 age group, people who loved black music. Jazz, soul, reggae, Asian and African were all on the playlist.

The force behind this project was Clement McLarty, who, with his forty-two pirate DJs, built up a large audience, broadcasting from secret locations in the heart of the city.

The station ran the risk of being busted by the police and one night, in the middle of a broadcast, two policemen were spotted, looking up at the windows. In ten minutes flat they had dismantled their equipment and sat waiting for the knock on the door. It never came but the fear of a two year jail sentence and the confiscation of their gear caused the group to close the station for three years.

After FTP resumed its operations, it grew slowly but surely as the team became increasingly professional, broadcasting twenty-four hours a day, seven days a week. Their equipment was cheap and sometimes the transmitter’s signal was so weak it failed to reach the road outside. Despite these difficulties, the station eventually built up an audience of 40,000 listeners.

In 1990, FTP obtained the approval of the Home Office and the necessary financial backing to set up a legitimate station. The next move was to find a suitable location from which to transmit its programmes.

The second floor of No. 25 Portland Square seemed an obvious choice. A sound-proof studio was constructed with all the latest recording equipment, together with a suite of administrative offices. The MP for the area at the time was William (later Sir William) Waldegrave. He was most enthusiastic for this new enterprise which he hoped would give a new confidence to the black community in St. Paul's.

Unfortunately, for many complex reasons, the radio station could not fulfil its professional ambitions and after a few years it was taken over by Galaxy Radio. This station remained at No. 25 until 1998, when it relocated to Baldwin Street. The recording studio was subsequently let to Attic Attack the same year.

Attic Attack Recording Studio was established by Pete Rowley in 1987 and has grown from a humble 8-track set-up to a fully digital 48-track, making use of the latest technology and computers.

The studio has a wide range of clients, mainly musicians from the Bristol area, although some come from further afield, including Europe and the USA. They include bands, singers and groups of many styles – rock, hip-hop, jazz, folk, classical, etc. There are also actors (some of whom are well known to TV viewers), doing advertising voice-overs, audio books and corporate work.

Pete Rowley runs the studio, produces and engineers the recordings and provides some of the keyboard parts. He has also written songs and music for dance theatre, film and radio advertisements.

No. 25 was to see more changes in its chequered history. In 1985, my husband had a desire to return to his roots. He had always had an empathy with St. Paul's and its colourful past and, as the square emerged from the shadows, its potential suggested to us that it could become our home. We were the first permanent residents of the square for many years.

Eleven years later we were suddenly no longer alone. One morning we noticed considerable activity outside No. 21. This house had been unoccupied for a number of years after Photobition, manufacturers of plastic signs, had vacated the premises.

The new owners were Harry Stealey and Thomas Flight of Video-Tec Group PLC. They had started their production company in Park Street in 1991, making training videos involving a variety of subjects. If a company wanted to send out a message, Video-Tec's short but comprehensive videos were the perfect answer. Their clients were so delighted with the results of these tapes that they requested copies. Eventually, they too ran out of space.

Because they had worked in the centre of Bristol, Harry and Thomas had no desire to move out to a trading estate. Instead, they searched for a perfect setting for their new premises. Chancing upon Portland Square and seeing the 'For Sale' sign on No. 21 they knew instantly that they had found what they were looking for. The square was stylish, convenient, close to Broadmead and, in those days, had free parking.

They moved in and the larger premises enabled the company to expand further, so much so that they acquired a warehouse in Wilder Street and diversified into the duplication of CDs and DVDs.

Although the congregation of St. Paul's church was diminishing, weddings were still being held there. The three daughters of the Elliott family, Irene, Brenda and Edna, were all married in St. Paul's. Irene was married to Anthony Clapp on the 13th October, 1962 and Edna, the youngest in the family, was married on 1st October, 1966 to Roger Hooper. Both ceremonies were carried out by Rev. J.E. Viner.

Not only did the couples have to pay for their services, but heating and choir charges were added and if the church bells were rung there was a considerable bill to pay. The photo of Irene's wedding gives a sense of the imposing character of the church and also shows the glorious stained glass window.

The Elliott family had lived in Bishop Street and Edna and Roger, who had lived nearby, could recall a vibrant community with events taking place in the church hall, scouts and guides meetings and later a group for young wives.

The church finally closed its doors in 1988 and it was to be sixteen years before a new use was found for the building.

CHAPTER SIX

Rags to Riches

NEARLY TWO HUNDRED YEARS ELAPSED BEFORE BRISTOL WAS once again engulfed in a building frenzy comparable to that of the early nineteenth century. At the end of the twentieth century the developers turned their attention to the harbourside. This part of the river, once a bustling port, had become almost derelict. A few dredgers were used to keep the river free of silt and the *s.s. Great Britain*, in dry dock, was gradually being restored. Apart from the Watershed, Arnolfini and the Industrial Museum there was little activity in the area.

When Lloyds Bank decided to relocate its head office to Bristol this set off a spate of building along the banks of the floating harbour. Flats and houses sprang up and people realised that this could be an ideal place to live. River ferries became a necessary form of transport and when Millennium Square with its surrounding cinemas, bars and restaurants appeared, Bristol became one of the largest tourist attractions in the country.

Portland Square has benefited from these two periods of activity, built in the first phase and restored during the second.

The most important restoration project is that of St. Paul's church. Circomedia, in partnership with the Churches Conservation Trust, plans to convert the church, a Grade 1 listed building, into a thriving venue for community arts and a centre of excellence for circus. St. Paul's church has stood empty for fifteen years and has long been associated with drugs and prostitution. The Churches Conservation Trust is currently restoring the building, thanks to funding from the Heritage Lottery Fund.

Circomedia will equip the church with 'state of the art' facilities, including a full scale flying trapeze rig as well as other gymnastic and circus equipment. There will also be office facilities and a café separated from the main training space by a glass screen so that the local community can come and observe activities. The new centre will house classes, workshops, accredited training courses, festivals, performances and events and will encourage the positive use of the green spaces surrounding the church. It is hoped that the centre will open in autumn 2004.

The bells of St. Paul's church have an interesting history. The tower was originally designed to hold a ring of ten bells. However, only four bells were purchased, all cast by John Rudhall of Gloucester, two in 1792 and the 6th and tenor bells of the proposed ring in 1795. At the time the church was declared redundant in 1993 only the two 1795 bells were hung, the 1792 bells resting on the frame. Interestingly, only one of the 1792 bells would have been suitable as part of the ring of ten bells, the other bell being too small, too light and the wrong note.

The three lighter bells were removed from the church after it was made redundant, leaving the 26 cwt tenor as the clock bell. This now chimes out the hours across the square. One of the 1795 bells is to become the tenor of the proposed ring of eight bells at St. James in Sydney, Australia.

More and more churches in Australia are installing bells for English-style bell ringing and the lighter of the two 1792 bells has been acquired for the church of St. John in Wagga Wagga, New South Wales.

The remaining bell has been installed in the church of St. Michael and All Angels in Buckland Dinham, Somerset. Its ring of six bells had been unringable from the 1950s until the completion of an ambitious restoration programme in1994 to replace the rotten bell-frame and augment to eight bells. The St. Paul's bell is now the 2nd of the ring.

In 1948 the clock in the tower of the church was dedicated as a memorial to the two world wars, with the words 'War Memorial 1948' inscribed on its face.

Another exceptional restoration was that carried out at No. 27 by June Burrough. Although the house had been occupied by both private families and businesses, the various owners had valued its architectural features and had made only superficial changes to the interior of the building.

When June bought the house from the English Corrugating Paper Co. Ltd. on the 20th June, 2001, she had no idea what an architectural treasure she had acquired and the first stage of the restoration, funded by June and Triodos Bank took a year to complete. On the 21st June, 2002 the Pierian Centre was opened and plans to restore the front of the building, with English Heritage funding, are now under way.

Corinthian capital at No 27.
Drawing by Terry Burke

In the early 1980s, June Burrough was company and stage manager of the Bristol Old Vic. In 1982 she became a freelance management consultant, personal development trainer and life coach. With these skills June spent eighteen months in Australia, leaving England in 1991 and travelling extensively. Whilst there, she thought of the idea of building a centre with an holistic approach to personal growth and learning, relevant to working and non-working life.

Towards the end of her stay, June was adopted by an Aboriginal community in

Arnhem Land in Northern Australia. Living there for five weeks was the inspiration of the Pierian Centre. This centre challenges modern day working practices which can stunt a person's potential.

When June first entered No. 27, the sense of calm which pervaded the building persuaded her that she had found not only her place of work but also her home.

The courses in the Pierian Centre range from management training and time management, through laughter yoga, Tibetan overtone chanting, pilates and many more. Alongside these, the Centre is also used by blue chip companies for meetings, hosts induction programmes for new deal trainees and is licensed for weddings.

One of the fastest growing enterprises in the square is Gordano Training. Funded by the government, it operates as an independent training provider through the Learning Skills Council and its aims are to help disaffected young people to reach their full potential. Through its training programmes they can achieve formal qualifications, develop personally, gain career experience and employment.

In September 2002 Gordano, one of eleven in the country, was chosen to pilot the new government Entry to Employment (E2E) programme and offices were found at 22-24 Portland Square.

At the same time Gordano made a successful bid for additional funding from the LSC to enable the internationally renowned artist and interior designer, Terence Wilson-Fletcher, who has worked extensively for royalty and heads of state, to set up a pilot scheme. He was interested in using creative activities to enable so-called unteachable youngsters to explore and develop practical skills.

The scheme was so successful that he set up an arts-based training programme at No. 25 Portland Square and called it Portlandsquare.com as another arm of Gordano Training. It offers a wide range of education-based courses including graphics, animation, photography, sculpture, web design and fine art.

The courses have enabled students to pursue career paths which they may never have considered, three have begun Foundation Art courses at FE colleges and another trainee is now in his second year at University reading Art. There have also been prestigious public art commissions in Bristol, one notable commission was to design a large installation including artwork and advance technology for the new Children's Hospital.

Portland Square has attracted two charities dedicated to helping children in need. In 2001 Shelter's 'Homeless to Home' moved into No. 34. This branch of Shelter deals specifically with families. The charity provides help with the move from temporary to permanent accommodation in order to avoid another period of homelessness, a cycle which occurs all too often when families are disrupted.

Help is given with rent arrears, filling in benefits forms, obtaining grants and liaising with local councils. Practical help is also given from fixing curtains and washing machines to help with decorating, gardening and advice on DIY.

Children are especially vulnerable in these conditions. Not only is their home life difficult but repeated change of school can lead to loss of friends and an inability to cope with the curriculum. Shelter has set up a play area at No. 34 and also a drama workshop.

The second charity is the National Association for Children of Alcoholics (NACOA) which moved into No. 25 in 2000 and relocated to No. 10 in 2002.

NACOA was founded in 1990 to address the problems of children growing up in families where one or both parents suffer from alcoholism or a similar addictive problem. The children can, of course, be any age and many adults also ring the free confidential helpline.

This helpline is manned by volunteers who wish to make a contribution to a worthwhile project. As well as providing a listening service they also have a website, respond to e-mail and letters, produce a quarterly newsletter and organise training programmes for volunteers.

NACOA's chief executive is Hilary Henriques and there is a formidable list of patrons including Fergal Keane OBE, Tony Adams MBE and Dr. Mo Mowlam.

Portland Square has once again become a magnet for young dispossessed girls. As happened in the early part of the twentieth century, when broken homes caused a migration of young women into the town centre, problems at the end of that century have given rise to a similar influx into the inner city.

Unfortunately, the simple solution of providing hostels in the area is no longer available. Over the past fifteen to twenty years, as drugs have become a major problem in St. Paul's, girls who have been drawn into the drug scene have found that prostitution can be a way to maintain their addiction.

There are a number of services in the area which give help and support to the women and in some cases their efforts have led to a complete change of lifestyle.

There are a number of commercial and professional operations in the square which help to maintain its diverse character; the Kilminster Financial Group at Portland House, and solicitors Allen & Partners at No. 5 and Henriques Griffiths at No. 18.

Four years ago in 2000 a company called Hotelscene moved into No. 17. The previous occupant was Sedgwick Healthcare Ltd. This firm had a call centre selling health insurance in the church hall which lies behind the house.

Hotelscene had relocated from Queen's Square where it had started two years earlier but had quickly outgrown its office accommodation. No. 17 was for sale and David Adams, the managing director, bought the property which was still in pristine condition. A few alterations and additions were necessary, such as replacing the strip lighting with elegant chandeliers and installing a free-standing mezzanine floor in the church hall.

Hotelscene is a 'business to business' operation, finding venues and booking hotel accommodation for firms holding conferences, events and seminars world wide. The firm also arranges full catering facilities for these events, using hi-tech equipment and, at the moment, has a staff of seventy-five.

The Portland Wine Bar was opened in the 1970s at No. 34 to cater for the growing number of office workers in the square. In the early nineties, under new management, the Wine Bar's image was given a radical overhaul. Gone was the sedate atmosphere of wining and dining and in its place appeared Cosies. Whilst still catering for its daytime clientele, in the evenings it became a venue for devotees of the rock scene.

The current owner of the restaurant, Martin Gibson, who is coincidentally married to a member of the Corrigan family, took over in October 2002. He acknowledges that the club scene has changed. The dozens of bars in Whiteladies Road have meant that, once again, Clifton has captured, if not the residents of Portland Square, some of its patrons.

Undaunted, Martin explains that he is following the same theory as the old management but evolving. He is offering tapas meals in the early evening and soon hopes to open at lunchtime on Saturdays and Sundays.

The restoration of the square together with government policy of regenerating inner city areas for residential use has attracted the attention of property developers. Three houses, Nos. 11, 12 and 14, which had stood empty for a number of years, have been transformed into luxury flats, complete with parking facilities. The accommodation is a mixture of studio and one and two-bedroom apartments. Nos. 26, 29, 30 and 31 all have planning applications pending for residential use.

Because of the quality of its architecture Portland Square, even at its lowest ebb, has always maintained its reputation as one of the great squares of Bristol. In the early stages of its long history, the square was a community with church and minister, family associations and no doubt close friendships.

New residents moving into the square have also expressed a desire to be part of a community. Paul and Elaine Robinson, who manage 'The Florist Ltd' on Bond Street, moved into No. 11 in June 2003. They were commuting from Bath but when they saw Portland Square they realised it was the perfect location.Because of its proximity to their place of work, the ease of parking in the evenings and at weekends for family and friends and access to the delightful garden, there is every reason for them to stay.

Another new resident, Nick Pratt at No. 14, also has long term intentions. Nick manages the lounge bar at the Pam Pam in Clifton but says that Portland Square is the place to live. He sees it as an up and coming area with real character. He has been in the square since February 2003 and has no intention of moving.

All the residents, whatever their reasons for moving into the square, seem to echo the same concern. They do not wish the square to house a transient population where developers build small one-bedroom flats which discourage the growth of a community. Larger flats should be encouraged with perhaps a few shops in the very near vicinity to support the inevitable increase in population.

Judging by the enthusiasm expressed by the residents there is every prospect that Portland Square will once again become a true community. In that event, the square will have turned full circle.

BIBLIOGRAPHY

Alford, B.W.E. *WD & HO Wills and the Development of the UK Tobacco Industry 1786-1965*. Methuen and Co Ltd., London. (1973)

Craig, Edward *Gordon Craig: The Story of his Life*, Victor Gollancz, London. (1968)

Gomme, Andor, Jenner, Michael & Little, Bryan *Bristol: an architectural history* (1979)

Ison, Walter *The Georgian Buildings of Bristol*, Faber & Faber, Bath. (1952)

Manson, Michael *Riot: the Bristol Bridge Massacre of 1793*. Bristol Past & Present Press. (1997)

Mowl, Timothy *To Build the Second City*, Redcliffe Press, Ltd., Bristol. (1991)

Nabb, Harold *The Bristol Gas Industry 1815-1949.*

Priest, Gordon *The Paty Family*, Redcliffe Press, Ltd., Bristol. (2003)

Pryce, George *A Popular History of Bristol* (1861)

Smith, Veronica *Images of England, St. Paul's & St. Werburgh's*. Tempus Publishing, Ltd., Stroud. (1998)

Terry, Ellen *The Story of my Life*, Hutchinson & Co., London.

INDEX

ACKNOWLEDGEMENTS

My thanks to the Bristol Records Office for their advice and assistance in showing an absolute beginner how to access the secrets of the library.

My thanks also to Nick Thomas for his invaluable guidance as proof reader and editor.

I am also grateful to the following for their generosity in sharing with me the many fascinating details they have discovered of the square:

Richard Thompson	Tony Broad
Toni Demidowicz	Jim McNeill
George Demidowicz	Veronica Smith
Dr. M.J. Crossley Evans	Mary Wright
Robert Burgess	Sonia Elliman
Douglas Merritt	The Salvation Army

Finally to my husband, Julius, who put up with my disappearances into the archives with fortitude and good humour.